"Verbs that Move Mountains"

Essays and Interviews on Spoken Word Cultures Around the World

Edited by Claire Trévien

Sabotage Reviews

This edition was first published in 2018.

Sabotage Reviews

www.sabotagereviews.com

Copyright © 2018 Claire Trévien

ISBN: 1981523049
ISBN-13: 978-1981523047

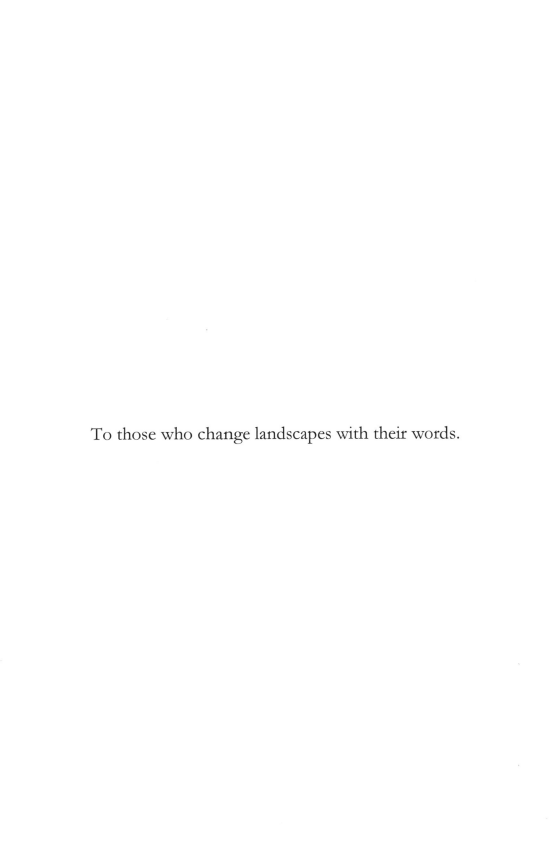

To those who change landscapes with their words.

have in common too the sense of community (poets seem to be the most social of the writing species), whether virtual or not, and examples of this can be found at all levels of professional development – from tentative amateurs to hardy pros.

At the time of penning this, the Watts/McNish argument is still raging within my online poetry circles, often bent on reducing 'page' and 'stage' poets to tired stereotypes I'd hoped we'd eviscerated at least half a decade ago. According to such arguments, the 'page' poets live in ivory towers writing stuffy verses about their mortgages and elbow patches, terrified of being assailed and destroyed. Meanwhile, the 'stage' poets are equally broadly stroked as ignorant iconoclasts, merrily leading their troupe of hapless fans into the volcano with them. Criticism on both sides often descends into identity assassination rather than genuine analysis of specific literary work. I suppose we better brace ourselves for several more decades of this before a new conflict is found. In the meantime, as Sophia Walker says in her interview: "The lit world better make way. We'll just keep coming".

The essays and interviews collected in this anthology will, I hope, provide an antidote to such tired arguments and push them in more intriguing directions.

Verbs that move mountains has been a while in the making and is a glimpse at the way practitioners and performers engage with spoken word around the world. There are attempted histories of specific scenes, hard looks at how to make spoken word a more accessible and open space in terms of sexuality, mental health, indigenous languages and more…. Academic analysis co-exists with personal reflections. Current topics, such as the ethics of honesty in slam poetry, or the very real dangers faced by many poets around the world, are also discussed. These essays give you snapshots of scenes from Singapore to New Zealand, and you might be surprised at how many of the spoken word communities included have created global ties through artist visits, festivals, and online resources. I found these voices dazzling and powerful, and I hope you do too.

Two late additions to the anthology came in the form of interviews – a glaring geographical hole I could not seem to fill was Central and South America. Lawrence Schimel came to the rescue here by introducing me to several authors. We were able to include Mexican poet Martín Rangel in time for the deadline and will feature future connections on the Sabotage Reviews website. I also couldn't resist including the force of nature that is Sophia Walker. Beyond being a globe-trotting poet, she is also the co-founder of an inspiring cross-continental project, The Spoken Word Theatre Foundation. I am so excited to see where this branch of spoken word takes us all.

Certainly, the anthology you see before you is imperfect in many ways, all anthologies are by default. There are geographical areas I hoped we could cover, there are untackled angles. Spoken Word is a multi-headed creature that continues to warp and evolve faster than I can type.

So, here's the thing: let's please see this book as the start of something rather than a final say. If anyone reading this anthology is inspired but feels unrepresented by it, get in touch. I'd love to see a series of these anthologies, with new editors at the helm of each, perhaps with a tighter geographical or thematic focus. My email is at the bottom of the introduction if you want to get in touch.

The title of the book comes from a quote found in South African Ingrid de Kok's beautiful poem 'Parts of Speech', and it is used with the kind permission of the author. I don't want to spoil the poem for any readers unfamiliar with it, but it felt too perfect not to be included.

Finally, this being a spoken word themed anthology, we made a YouTube channel of course, made up of videos suggested by the writers (or referenced in their essays). Check 'em out to extend the experience:

http://bit.ly/verbmountains

Claire Trévien
editor@sabotagereviews.com

we wondered: how might story contribute to rebuilding the spirit of the people?

> 'And so, I broke free. I no longer torment myself with constant weight-watching and dieting. Life is about joy, so I enjoy food and all that nourishes me in my life.' – Jill

And now it is April 2017. It's getting late on a Friday night and the evening is drawing to a close at *Exchange Christchurch (XCHC)* – a central city cafe and creative space. There are clusters of people chatting together, some with 'strangers' they have just met that night, reluctant to part and head home. Cafe staff are clearing tables with a smile and a welcoming presence that invites further conversation. Jill stands before me, seemingly taller and straighter than at the beginning of the evening; a light in her eyes, her face shining. 'I didn't know I could do that!' she declares. There is an energy about her, an infectious buzz, and I have the sense that she has just uncovered another layer of understanding of who she is, what her life story means and what she has to offer the world. Basking in her glow, I feel humbled and blessed to be a witness. Jill has just shared a story of 'breaking free'; free from a lifelong torment of weight-watching and dieting, to a world where her focus is joy, nourishment and fun. This was a story she had no idea she was going to tell when she stepped into the room earlier in the evening.

Jill's inspirational tale was the closing story at *Natural Born Storytellers*, a bi-monthly true-life tales event *The Story Collective* now hosts. It's become a popular regular event on our calendar – a line-up that also includes workshops, performances, story circles and international guest storytellers across both traditional and true-life storytelling. We have been fortunate to have hosted renowned tellers such as Dovie Thomason of the Lakota Kiowa Apache tradition (USA), Shonaleigh Cumbers who is the only surviving drut'syla of an ancient Jewish tradition (UK), peace and diversity activist Donna Jacobs Sife (Australia) and more. Our visitors generously stopping by on their travels through the country, have made a significant contribution in building a local community of oral storytelling and supporting our skill development.

Natural Born Storytellers is the brain child of Michael Kossew, a storyteller and community creative from London. I met Michael on a storytelling course in South Africa with the International School of Storytelling at the end of 2013. He told me about a monthly true-life tales event he was running in Camden Town. He was so inspiring and passionate about what he was doing that it stuck with me. Despite true-life tales being my ultimate personal challenge, something about what Michael was doing got under my skin and worked away at me. Then at the end of 2015 Camia Young, the Founding Director of *XCHC*, synchronistically shared that she loves storytelling and really wanted to support our work. It seemed like a Christchurch chapter of *Natural Born Storytellers* was demanding to be born and we just had to give it a go.

But would it work? Christchurch is renowned for its conservatism, frequently greeting the most accomplished artist with polite silence and restrained applause. Revealing personal stories about themselves in a public venue to a bunch of strangers might go down like a lead balloon in this town. What gave me hope was the *dance-o-mat*, another creative earthquake response, where people plug in their iPod to a converted washing machine and dance on an open-air stage complete with disco ball in vacant lots amid the destruction of the central city. General opinion said Christchurch folk don't dance, and certainly don't dance in public. Wrong! They *love* to dance dance-o-mat style with it becoming one of the most successful creative regeneration projects the city has seen.

Fortunately, *XCHC* is all about taking risks like this, giving artists a safe place to experiment, and where failing is okay. It's a community space in a converted warehouse near the fatally damaged sports stadium at the edge of Christchurch's central city. Like *The Story Collective*, *XCHC* was established in response to the earthquakes of 2010 and 2011. The vision of *XCHC* is cultivating a creative ecology and providing a space for artists and creatives to gather and work, a replacement for their previous haunts destroyed by the earthquakes. The *XCHC* team supported our experimental first steps with the *Natural Born Storytellers* concept by inviting us to be part of their free Friday night community event programme in their cafe-exhibition space. And so, a co-creative partnership came into being and we launched in February 2016.

While our evenings are based on Michael's *Natural Born Storytellers* concept from London, we have adjusted the format to suit our

4. THE TIES THAT BIND: COMMUNITIES OF PRACTICE IN GRASSROOTS SPOKEN WORD IN THE SCOTTISH CENTRAL BELT.

Rachel McCrum

I arrived in Edinburgh as a fresh(ish) green thing in the spring of 2010. The plan was to spend the next four years working on a PhD in the School of Management at a prestigious Scottish university, researching communities of practice in Scottish craft. Reader, I did not finish that PhD. Instead, I became first curious about, then involved in, then deeply embedded in the spoken word/performance poetry scene. Between 2011 and 2016, I moved from a tentative participation on the edges of the spoken word community to making a full-time career as a poet, performer, promoter and workshop facilitator for the last two years of my time in Edinburgh (I moved to Montreal in January 2017. That's another story).

The original, short-lived PhD used – would have used - the theory of communities of practice to investigate craft in Scotland. The craft element has fallen by the wayside, but the literature of communities of practice may be used as a frame for ideas of access, participation and development in the spoken word community/scene/milieu in the Central Belt (i.e. the large urban centres of Edinburgh and Glasgow) in Scotland during this time.

By framing spoken word in Edinburgh and Glasgow first as a community and then, further, as a community of practice, we may gain some insight into how such a community functions; how participants and practitioners learn and develop; and how a community can accommodate change within itself, as new members grow in experience and expertise. How do participants in the community talk to one another, support, dispute and negotiate with one another? What does success look like, and is it important? What function does the community itself serve? And how do the individual and community practices relate to one another?

Community knowledge is often tacit or implicit: by making these interactions more explicit, we may make also make more apparent how people may access that community; how we share knowledge and learning within it; and how we increase the visibility of this community – of the practice of spoken word – in the outside world.

I'd like to look at how new writers and performers access the 'scene'; how they gain credibility, reputation, status and even authority. Looking at some of the regular event series that ran between 2011 and 2016, I'd like to understand more about how the rules of the community are set and understood, and who is setting them (if such rules even exist). Finally, I'd like to try to differentiate between the classifications of grassroots and professional, even in a field as unstructured as spoken word.

One of the notable defining characteristics of the spoken word community in Scotland between 2011 and 2016 was its self-generated, grassroots, DIY nature, perhaps more akin to a punk movement than a literary one. Rather than the traditional literary networks of publishers, prizes, academic posts, invitations to festivals, inclusion in journals and attention from literary criticism, and lacking even the gatekeeper institution of something like Apples & Snakes (the funded spoken word organisation that operates across England and Wales, setting up professional development, mentoring opportunities, touring, workshops training and standardized fees for artists), the community members really are making it up themselves.

A few caveats. Firstly, for the sake of brevity and sanity, and to avoid entanglement in those endless semantic arguments of what constitutes 'spoken word' or 'performance poetry', take as the basis those events where poets and writers stand on stages and deliver words that they have written to a live audience, with an intent to perform. 'Grassroots' in this case refers to event series unaffiliated to any larger literary institution; usually not for profit and/or run by practitioners who are not – and do not have the intention – of making a living from it. Either Open Mic (i.e. anyone can sign up to perform) or curated, they are also concerned with ideas of access and community, of providing opportunities for new speakers.

The essay draws on my own experience in Scotland at this time, and thus is subjective, individual and above all, descriptive rather than prescriptive. I'm using my own experiences of a particular time in a particular environment to ask some questions, and describe events that occured.

It's also worth clarifying that this isn't an attempt to contribute to the academic literature on communities of practice, but rather a loose application of this theory to the real-life experiences of being within the spoken word community in Scotland during this time. There is, without doubt, a full academic thesis to be written about this, by someone else, at some point. I ask in advance the forgiveness of the community for the vagueness of this piece, and of borrowing from our collective experiences.

I've found this – my - spoken word community to be full of contrary buggers, independently minded outliers, wilful rebels and *thrawn* souls[9], and I write those words with love. This may be true of any community of artists but, I would argue, particularly true so of a group who relies on organic growth such as spoken word. Lacking academic or artistic institutions – no conservatoires, theatre schools, marketing departments, training for us! - the paths to professionalism, to learning, to 'success' are not pre-determined, and so we tramp our own. This might be something to be examined, discussed for the future. For the time and place that this essay deals with, we were informally organised, tacit acknowledgers of unspoken rules – but we were organised, to a degree. As such, it can be called a community.

What defines a community of practice?

The term 'community of practice' is most often attributed to academics Jean Lave and Etienne Wenger, and their study of situated learning

---

[9] *thrawn* is an Ulster-Scots word meaning 'contrary'.

published in 1991. Although the concept had been cited in texts before this, Lave and Wenger's book outlined certain characteristics deemed typical of and specific to a community of practice. It also placed the idea of communities of practice within the sphere of learning, of knowledge sharing and of development.

Communities of practice are commonly defined by three characteristics: the domain, the community and the practice. To paraphrase Wenger:

(I) **Domain** – a community of practice will have an identifiable domain of interest. Members of the community will be identifiable by their shared commitment to and competence in this domain and, therefore, distinguishable from non-members.
This leads to questions: who defines the domain? How do you become a member? Who defines competence and commitment and more, who quantifies or qualifies the contribution of this commitment?

(II) **Community** – the community will be identifiable as such because of the interactions that occur within it; there will be joint activities, discussions. These interactions may be held in person or online; they may be intermittent or regular; formal or informal; genial or quarrelsome, conclusive or inconclusive. They may entail an active seeking of advice, a sharing of resources, repertoire, vocabulary, experiences, stories, tools; of ways to address recurring problems in the practice; of mentoring, of discussion around experience, etc. The communities themselves may be intentional or incidental but one way or another, *'beliefs and behaviours are acquired through social behaviour and collaboration.' [Wenger]*.

(III) **Practice** – the members of a community of practice will have not just a shared interest but a shared practice: they are practitioners.

Grassroots spoken word in Scotland as a community of practice

If we're to define grassroots spoken word as a community of practice, then, we could examine the following specific situations.

Domain and community - The domain of this community is found in an environment which allows practitioners to get onto a stage and speak words to a live audience; in all the work that goes into creating, supporting and maintaining those environments; and in the discussions around how they are best managed, whether in the pub after a show or, as is possibly more usual these days, in online spaces such as Facebook groups or discussions on Facebook threads. Where once bulletin boards or dedicated online forums would have existed for such groups, I would argue most of these discussions take place on Facebook, which is positive (the sense of open access, immediacy) and negative (the lack of structured or formal discussion space; the lack of archiving and subsequent risk of missing out on a current debate or discussion; lack of moderation or guidelines for engagement).

Demonstrations of commitment, competence – means of contributing – could be arguably those of being artist, audience member, promoter and/or contributing to real time and online debate.

The most commonly used public forum, the 'Poetry & Spoken Word in Scotland' Facebook group currently boasts 2, 587 members, with at least daily posts for upcoming events, sharing of videos and opportunities.[10] The online group is also interesting in that it has clearly defined and explicitly stated rules for what can and cannot be posted on the group page:

'YES: EVENT SPAM -VIDEO POEMS

NO: TEXT POEMS . ✖ ABUSE . ✖ SHITTY BEHAVIOUR . ✖

What began as a planning group for Glasgow poetry and spoken word promoters and performers.... has become Scotland's largest spoken word group on Facebook. Yaldi!

YOU ARE WELCOME HERE please abide by the rules. Extended rule guff explanation fodder is below....

....

WHAT DO YOU MEAN BY "ABUSE AND SHITTY BEHAVIOUR"
Basically anything the admins deem unacceptable. We Are Always Watching. Our Decision Is Final.

---

[10] http://bit.ly/SpokenWordScotland

WHY WE ASK THAT YOU DON'T POST TEXT POEMS

This isn't really a group for posting written poetry in. It's a fast-moving, community-driven event-sharing and   discussion group for LIVE poetry and spoken word. So we accept videos of poems being read, but not written   poems.

One exception we make to that is video/audio poems - as these can serve as tasters/previews for events and   performers. If you want to record a piece and share it on Soundcloud or YouTube and re-post, that's fine! But the admins will have to delete text poems and attached documents when they are posted.

Please don't be offended if your post disappears.

Cheers
The Admins'

These rules have been – at least tacitly – accepted by the community for conduct within this group and thus may give some indication to a collectively agreed definition of the practice: the emphasis on 'LIVE poetry and spoken word'.

Interestingly, within the Scottish spoken word community 2011 to 2016, it could be argued that the majority of conversations centre around the practice of anything but the poetry/performance itself. Conversations around building platforms, gender balance and diversity, safe spaces, pay (and lack of it), good and bad experiences of performing, queries about how to find workshop work, to apply for residencies are common. It is rarer to find conversations – or public conversations, certainly – about the specifics of a poem or a performance, in-depth critical examinations of particular work, or sharing of workshop resources, etc. This is partially, I think, due to a healthy awareness of competition (particularly in terms of workshops) and partially due to the sensitivity of a small community. So, while to become a 'member' of the community, you must perform in front of a live audience at least once, you are possibly likely to spend more time talking about logistics, moral decisions of programming, fair pay than about the 'art' itself.

the model before we roll it out, and we want to earn a reputation for doing exactly what we say we will. That takes patience, it takes time, and it takes a very clear idea of total levels of funding that we're playing with. The Lagos pilot project was supported by the British Council in partnership with Writers' Centre Norwich, UK as part of the International Literature Showcase, and while that was incredible, we are now in the process of cementing funding for 2018 and beyond. The enthusiasm from the global scene is there. The commitment from us is there. Our only limitation is money.

Do you have any highlights to share from your visit to the Lagos International Poetry Festival?

The entire Lagos International Poetry Festival was a highlight.

I came across some truly great writers. Personally, I was most struck by the bravery. I think oftentimes we are able in the UK scene to have the luxury of having spoken word be a form of entertainment if we want it to be. In many other countries, it is always activism. Because so much is taboo. Any form of speaking out can be taboo. We had people creating LGBT work in our workshops. To put that in context, one of the participants had been stabbed three weeks prior for being gay, another had been kidnapped and tortured over a three-day period for having written a blog post about being gay. And there we were in a room where they could speak freely, create freely, and where every other participant supported and applauded them. Yes, we have security concerns. Yes, locations and access and who is in ear-shot are all things we must be very, very careful with in these situations, and we are hugely mindful of what protection we can and can't give (and of what might happen when we, and indeed the privilege we bring with us, leave) but being a small part of providing that room, that space where such work could be made and aired, was one of the best things I've ever done in my career.

It's great to see spoken word and theatre intersecting more formally. How would you personally define Spoken Word Theatre?

The hardest thing Dike, Katie and I found when planning our workshops was trying to define the genre! It's popping up all over the world completely independently, and it's appearing in a variety of forms. I'm not sure I can tell you what spoken word theatre is, I think we are all deciding and defining that, globally, at the moment. I think the best answer we can currently give is that it is the combining of theatrical elements with spoken word writing. So staging matters, there's blocking, there is probably some element of characterization, … It is hard to currently lay-out 'this is spoken word theatre' without feeling like I'm limiting people in the very act of inventing this new thing. But I can tell you what it isn't: it's not a loose set. It's not turning up to the Edinburgh Fringe with your same 12 poems you do all over your hometown all year long, loosely thrown together with some intros. Those come up every year, and that's fine, there's a space for that. But that is not spoken word theatre. I'd even hesitate to call that a show, that's a poetry set. Those are great, too, they're just not what we're interested in.

Based on the highly scientific research that is reading your occasional status on Facebook you seem to be almost constantly on a plane, performing from one country to the next. To quote a recent one: '4 weeks, 4 continents, 7 countries, 1 very tired me'. Sounds exhausting! Do you have any tips for intrepid performers trying to juggle gruelling schedules?

Buy an aeropress. It is only recently that I've graduated to the nice hotels side of life. Before that, it was Megabus and people's floors all the way. Aeropress was my godsend. If you have only slept intermittently for three hours on a hardwood floor and you still need to nail your show that night, good coffee is a non-negotiable. Aeropress is good, easily transportable, easily made coffee. Get a good frequent flyer programme, the miles add up fast. And because when people book you from overseas you don't get to choose the carrier, pick a programme that works across as many airlines as possible. Otherwise, google local manners. What is and isn't polite changes very quickly as you travel, and news of your behaviour always travels more quickly than news of your work.

The last tip…. just remain aware of your privilege. Know when you're doing something only you can do because you're white. Or male. Or straight. Or able bodied. Especially know when you're in a country where you have the safety of being able to say something (very carefully and gently) that someone else can't say. I can't go to Abu Dhabi lit fest, or to

6. ALLOWED TO BE ANGRY, OLIVE SKINNED AND YOUNG: HOW BEING A PALESTINIAN SPOKEN WORD POET CHANGED ME

Alice S. Yousef

Ramallah nights hadn't been chilly in years, but I was trembling. Mid-May, the humdrum of winter behind me, the shake of my leg wasn't caused by the formal, thin black trousers I had on. A few feet away from my chair, the microphone seemed to shake too, carrying the same weight I suddenly had on my chest. A full house for my first poetry night performance meant either I swallowed my tongue or spat out the wrong words. I did neither, when I held the microphone in my hands the shaking stopped.

Stepping down from the stage, I did not realize my life would change dramatically.

Not only was it my first performance in front of a crowd filled with my university instructors, friends, family and HBO Def-Jam superstar Suheir Hammad, performing under the umbrella of Palfest, the Palestine Literature Festival, but also it was the highlight of ending a long workshop.

In the late winter months of 2010, New York based poet Remi Kanazi teamed up with the Palestine Writing Workshop to teach a spoken word poetry workshop, the first of its kind in Palestine. Regardless of its known history of storytelling, well-derived fiction and rich poetry, Palestine did not have any formal or near formal teaching of creative writing. University students, young writers or poets had to carve their way out on their own assisted by their language skills, lucky encounters and the encouragement of family and friends. In 2009, the Palestine Writing Workshop [now a local NGO working on literary culture in Palestine], started its activities hosting international writers to teach and hone skills of students and artists alike with basic creative writing techniques. I was one of their first students.

Fourteen students, then attending Birzeit University, would flock around the round table in one of the oldest houses in the town, sit and write in utter quiet. The quiet was only broken by feeble attempts at capturing, in a few words, poetry. I, like many others, wrote in English. Before the first free-write, Remi asked one thing: 'be yourself, that's what matters most. Spoken word is a vehicle to give you voice'.

Graciously, with his clever dark humor, Remi left us to indulge before sharing the written work began. The end results of each exercise were different; some wrote about love, some wrote about insecurities, day-to-day activities. We swam the currents of generality until one evening an exercise faced our collective fear: write about what it feels like to live under occupation. Having never consciously needed to face this reality on paper, there was a good five-minute-long silence in the room, combined with confused glances. How could we write about something so emotionally substantive, in less than fifteen minutes?

Needless to say, we all tried to write part and parcel poems, diary-like, rhyming poems, poems invoking ancestors, lands occupied or generic feelings of hindered safety. The short poems were like punches of immediate emotions, there was no room for hiding behind words we feared. Blood poured in the poems, there were bodies, rocks, doves, olive-groves, walls and a twisted sense of anger that had been granted for us safe to use by spoken word: a tool of change, a voice that's not to be silenced. YouTube was our greatest sources of inspiration, having not had any exposure to the hip/hop culture (other than watching DAM the lead Palestinian Hip-hop band rap). It was a remarkable revelation to watch how several international artists bound their frustration in words and presented these to the world. The themes we covered had without our knowledge been filtering into the general defiance and rage present collectively within contemporary Palestinian literature, sentiments also mirrored in international literatures where subjugation, fear, oppression and negation of one's identity were very prominent. The poem I scratched out that day I still keep in an old notebook that I look into whenever I need a reminder of where the unveiling of my sharp poems really began.

The depth of this question was very evident in Remi's last exercise, having established a safe platform. Round mid-May, all fourteen of us would eventually find ourselves facing a crowd and a microphone answering one final question: who are you? What makes you different?

The power of that May night and the workshop was in the answers. Collectively, the group I was part of ranged in gender, interests, and age between 18 to 22, very young, seemingly inexperienced college students. It was staggering to see more anger than fear in our words. We were hot-blooded, not because of the molds we were set to cast and wear politically, but because our youth was marred by experiences of war, injustice, manifestations of oppression, insecurity and constant questioning for one sense of identity. Too many times we had bordered the definition, but nothing was clear to us. We had fine lines we knew we could individually and collectively never cross but we all had a final line we could not overlook; of youth marked by an experience that is generally unmatched elsewhere in the world. This realization and the raised platform changed us dramatically.

Much of the detail of these sessions now group in my mind between fact and memory; I recall most moments with clarity because the search for answers was remarkably singular, essentially collective. I, like others was angry but that experience was unique: between the push-ups, laughter, tears, voice projection exercises I had found a voice. My anger had found a way to leave me.

*****

For Palestinians, the question of identity revolves around many factors one of which is one's national spirit regardless of passport or geographic location. This spirit carries steadfastness at its core. In the short time span after I graduated the workshop, a growing trend of 'open mic' nights started to establish around the city of Ramallah, the country's second central city, a cultural hub receptive of languages, modern-style cafes and experimentation with forms of standardized literary practices. In a society that was community-based, these voices or nights could have backfired on organizers. Surprisingly, the support was staggering.

I soon found myself setting up for these poetry nights with friends who wrote into different genres and in both Arabic and English. The cafes or cultural centers would be teeming with family members and friends who would proudly show up to support, the set up was easier than expected: mutual understanding of putting up a microphone without harming the business. It only took one shout-out of thank you after performing or on the mike to feel well received amongst friends and cafe owners. Gradually, these poetry nights became well attended by the community starting from personal close circles into strangers attending and reading.

The crowds would be our next safe-zone. Generally, there was no restriction on themes or participants, as long as respect for public space, no (unnecessary) swearing onstage or over-running other performers with long pieces rules were respected, the nights went fine. Slowly, there was more than rage into the poetry: there was a continued sense of hope and steadfastness. It was the same time period that coincided with various turbulences in the country, relatively the same time when poet Rafeef Zeyadeh's "We Teach Life" started to take the country and the internet by storm. For a while, every teenager who had seen Zeyadeh's performance wanted to be in her shadow.

At this time, most Palestinian poets and spoken word artists were trying to figure out where they stand locally and internationally.

A few months down the road from this period, I found myself in the same shoes as my peers in front of a different microphone in a room where a handful of the audience were my friends, where I could barely make eye contact with the front row of the audience. Overhead lights had blinded me, and the vast room was warmer than usual with a mixture of age and gender in the room. By chance and choice, I was speaking in the voice of many Palestinians at the renowned Fringe Festival. Playing the two stages was very different, yet quite raw. I never expected the audience to be so moved by the experience of listening to me, in an accent, narrating the history of my refugee grandfather and the town where my cousin's classmate was shot to death at sixteen years of age. Language was never an issue, I wrote in English regardless of where I was, despite the poetic nature of Arabic yet I never resisted my native tongue. The interplay between the languages cast my work, as did other Palestinians in a grey area in between the two tongues. As if it was my first poetry night, the microphone seemed to shake: this time my poems where reaching a new locality larger than my own understanding.

This formation of identity carried me forward to other performances, one at the Poet's House in New York late through 2016. Having been in the States over a long period of time, within a politically charged atmosphere of changes, the conversations I had with friends were largely centered around how a certain literature can fall into a shade of a color where 'brown, black, white' were more than generic adjectives to describe a state of a culturally-infused work: mine would be a shade of rising olive skin. Yes, I was paler than most Palestinians, yet the rage, frustration, challenges, and changes of my area infused into the pieces read on stage. It was as if I came to terms with my own paleness, and poetic tongue, being naturally born into a nation that is primarily olive-skinned. A nation where poetry read in cafes wasn't for once related to your age, aspirations or dreams but where your identity: the color of its fold, the color of your features, determined how easy it was for you to cross a border or speak in someone's name.

****

Social media has been leaving its marks globally and in Palestine, the situation isn't too different. With the rise of new social media's global effect and its choices of one's preferences, I arrived at a sponsored advert for a Facebook page called Sard (Arabic for narration). The description box, interestingly offered a platform for free expression. The organizer of the Sard collective was a young poet a few years my senior who invited me to their first event which was set up in cooperation with Aik Saath (U.K) in a step toward supporting a spoken word community in Palestine.

Upon entering the Sakakini Cultural Center, where the monthly themed poetry night is held, I felt out of place. Not because of the fairy-lights, well-assembled decoration and ready audience but more because I was stepping into a room full of youth who looked like they were freshmen, many of whom actually were. I was amongst the only mid-twenties performers attending and reading. While the collective started with family and friends supporting performers, aspiring artists started joining the collective and became regulars with their own crowd sitting attentively on the edge of their seats waiting for the poems. The monthly sessions are now awaited for, and joined by the country's leading writers who make guest appearances to read and encourage the young generation to carry on with their poetic practice and in both languages Arabic and English to open up the space of expression.

Sard is currently a revival of all the spoken word poetry traditions present in the country. A collective of young, olive-skinned, realists and dreamers who are passionate about their words and artistry. Sard is primarily based in Ramallah city, where poetry nights are usual unlike areas in the northern and southern governorates of Palestine. Many Palestinians cannot access Jerusalem, for that, Sard has been growing its own audience. For a minute, I was blown away by the amount of youth attending the sessions until it hit me, I had started at that same very age.

The years of being a performer in Palestine made me note that the Palestinian spoken word community is diverse, in theme, languages and expression. Unlike storytelling, which has been passed down from one generation to the other, Palestinian spoken word is largely infused with realist pessimism, shaded with the many faces of identity and is still very young in experience and training. The lack of formal workshops, resources or grants to be channeled into this creative field leaves poets fending off for themselves to make a name. This has hindered further development on the 'experimentation' nature since poets are still fighting for a platform where they can be heard and taken seriously for not 'ranting'. Yet, this simplicity of set-up, allows the verse to be simple, whilst loaded with meaning and the new technology gives poetry a medium through social media and blogging.

What Sard has been teaching me over the last couple of months is that the younger generation lacks no guidance, all they need is a space that contains them. Used to fighting for every single right on a daily basis, the youth of Palestine and their work struggles to find its identity. For now, our poetry uses the platforms we are granted, from a small room filled with close relatives and friends onto a world stage. Young, olive-skinned, and angry poets are fighting for words to lift them up.

From an audience's distance I usually sit and applaud the younger poets before I join them behind a microphone that seems to rattle from time to time with loaded words and my shaky hands. Many times, I cannot help feeling like it's my first time ever on stage, playing like a broken record over and over in my head.

improve upon the genius of the empty page, and listen to the words floating in the spaces between me and Johannesburg, between Grahamstown and Rhini. As 12th century Chinese poet Yang Wan Li says, 'the poet does not go in search of the poem, the poem comes in search of the poet'.[22] (I wonder how many of us really do listen to those spaces.)

My stay in the Eastern Cape, in Grahamstown was a third eye-opening experience because the Xhosa I grew up knowing in Soweto is different from the Xhosa that is spoken 'eKoloni'. And to come across poets who write poetry in Xhosa, different from what I thought I knew as Xhosa poetry. I was amazed to listen to poets like Mxolisi Nyezwa, Mangaliso Welcome Buzani, Simphiwe Nolutshungu and Ayanda Billie whose poetry is strong on and off the page, and very emotional, whether the poets themselves read it to an audience or someone else does. The way they are able to use their home language, to make it sound quiet yet loud through underlining tones in their poetry.

There is music in every language, and since the English language has become an integral part of our culture, like the Jamaicans, South Africa has its own sounds and tones when speaking the English language. For example, when asking someone for directions, one would answer, 'I don't know but I am sure it's on the next street' or when someone is getting off a taxi, 'short left after robot'.

When the Peruvian poet, César Vallejo said, 'And what if after all the words, the word itself does not survive'[23] , I took it literally and had a midlife crisis thinking, what's the point of doing all this if the word is not going to survive. Later I got to realize after long conversations with my supervisors that it's not about the word he is talking about rather the language and how we as writers should push the envelope, and create new tones and meanings in language with the word. This is not British English, we are not British, we are South Africans and so is our English, and this is not Lesotho nor Botswana, yet we have our own register of seSotho and seTswana. I respect a writer, who will push the envelope when writing in isiZulu and show how isiZulu can be used creatively and expanded, as opposed to a writer writing in either Tsonga or tshiVenda or Afrikaans and making a mess of their own beautiful and musical language simply because they want to affirm their blackness, or their whiteness, and have no poetry in their writing whatsoever, ultimately, improving nothing on the blank

---

[22] Yang Wan Li, *The Art of Writing: Teachings of the Chinese Masters*, translated and edited by Tony Barnstone and Chou Ping (Shhambhala, 1996).

[23] Cesar Vallejo in Robert Bly, *Leaping Poetry* (University of Pittsburg Press, 1975).

page.

My time on the course opened my ears to voices I never knew about. Alex La Guma's *And A Threefold Cord* is descriptive writing on steroids, modimo!, the way his images jump off the page, I could smell the rain and hear the cry of a woman whose house is burning to the ground with her children still inside.[24] In Aimé Césaire's *Return to my Native Land*, I could see the child 'whose voice lost its mind in the marshes of hunger', I could feel the scent of Pale Street on my skin, and I could hear the sound of the ringing bells in William Carlos Williams' poem 'Catholic Bells'.[25]

I have felt, saw and still see how words capture my imagination, transport me in and out of my senses. One moment I am crying and the next I am laughing out loud. This happens to me with some words on stage and on the page. I listen with more than just my ears and eyes. Spanish poet Federico García Lorca says, 'If I am a poet by the grace of god, and of the devil, then I am a poet by the grace of hard work and technique'.[26]

So, before I write, I listen and wait patiently for the words to come find me, and when they do, they burst out of me. As the American poet Charles Bukowski says, 'if it is not bursting out of you, then don't do it'.[27]

Every poem has come to me through sound, before I could begin to write it down. And I have found that, when I begin to write, the page slows down the tempo of the poem, and I listen to how the words want to come out regardless of grammar, and regardless of whether they make sense or not. After I have gone through this process, I feel very relieved; it is as if a weight has been lifted off my shoulders. And then weeks later, when I revisit the poem, to type it out, I begin another process of editing. I come to the poem with a clear sense of mind, and when I transfer the raw material into a word.doc, I look at what needs to be typed and what needs to be left in my notepad, I become a sculptor chipping off the unwanted spaces to bring out the sculpture in the wood. And when it comes to performing that poem, the poem itself will tell me how it wants to be voiced, and this, becomes another level of editing, working on a plane of rhythm, tone and timing. When on stage about to perform a poem for the

---

[24] Alex La Guma, *And A Threefold Cord* (Kilptown, 1964).
[25] William Carlos Williams, 'Catholic Bells', http://bit.ly/2qSB846; Aimé Césaire, Return to My Native Land (Penguin Books 1968)
[26] Federico García Lorca, *The Selected Poems of Federico García Lorca*, edited by Donald M. Allen (New Directions, 2005).
[27] Charles Bukowski, 'So you want to be a writer', http://bit.ly/2qTvxdN

first time after weeks of learning it to the point where you recite it in your sleep, somehow the energy of the audience adds to the energy of the poem.

I have found that a lot of poems I perform on stage don't come out exactly the way I wrote them, and I don't mean that, the poem I wrote is different to the poem on stage, no. I mean that, the energy of the poem becomes so alive on stage, that the poem takes control of everything, forcing me to leap from the conscious to the subconscious, and when this is happening, I can hear my self subconsciously blocking out lines from the poem that I had learnt and written, but at that moment, the poem is editing itself to exactly what it wants to say, and using my voice to say what it needs to say. When this happens, all I can do is to allow myself to feel what the poem is doing to me. This is the energy of the word on stage that the poem brings to the page, the energy of the historian lion writing his or her story.

Looking at all the years I have been performing poetry, I still get very nervous every time I must get on stage, so much that I ask myself, why am I doing all of this? And then I recall what my mother once said to me:

'my son, if you are not happy about how someone treated you, don't bottle it in, just tell them how you feel about what they did, because if you don't and keep quiet, that person will carry on living their lives and you will not be able to, and will be stuck in that miserable feeling they put you through'.

So, for every performance, from the page to stage or from the stage to the page, I am 'breaking a silence that had to be overcome'.[28] .

When someone says to me, 'I write I don't perform', I think to myself, 'if only this punk knew', that my body is the stage and my tongue is the page, and that I am writing as we speak.

My father Matsemela Manaka says,

'Let us create and talk about life
Let us not admire the beauty
But peruse the meaning
Let art be life
Let us not eye the form

But read the content

---

[28] Adrienne Rich, ibid.

Let creativity be a portrait of one's life'.[29]

---

[29] Matsemela Manaka, *Return of The Amasi Bird*, edited by Tim Couzens and Essop Patel (Raven Press, 1982).

8. EDINBURGH VERSUS AUSTIN: POETRY SLAMS AND ETHICS

Catherine Wilson

Whilst studying for my English Literature and philosophy degree at the University of Edinburgh, I have had the pleasure of interacting with the Scottish spoken word scene in many different capacities. I spent a year purely as an audience member who did not write poetry. Then, from 2014-2015, I was a performer without the behind-the-scenes organisational point of view. Now, I organise nights in Edinburgh and Glasgow: from free student open mics, to paying showcases at one hundred seater venues and a fair share of competitive poetry slams.

The scene itself has always been bursting with support and community spirit. In January I, and a few other students, won a place representing our university at C.U.P.S.I. in Austin, Texas. C.U.P.S.I. is a national competition, which hosted sixty-seven university teams of four to five poets in 2016. It was created by Robb Thibault in 2001, and has since gone on to dominate most of the spoken word poetry on YouTube with authors like Patrick Roche and Lily Myer gaining five million online views and the channel that films it, Button Poetry, having 600,000 subscribers. These well-viewed authors go on to publish work and tour, so this online attention, and the competition itself, is no casual thing.

But Team Edinburgh had to get to America first. Whilst we were budgeting with constant spreadsheets, meetings, drafting and redrafting emails, poets from across the Scottish scene donated, performed at fundraisers for free, promoted our trip and generally did everything they could to encourage us.

People really 'came out of the woodwork' to help us try and achieve our goal. Luckily, we did! In April 2016 we competed in America's *College and University Poetry Slam Invitational* in The University of Texas at Austin.

As a philosophy student, my main area of interest has been ethics: especially how communities come to form ethics, whether explicitly and openly decided or written down rules, or whether they just remain somewhat unspoken. In this essay I hope to analyse the differences I noticed from my glimpse of America from my Edinburgh based perspective. I will openly admit, firstly, that my experience of American slam, whilst intense, did only last 3-4 days. That experience, and with what I have heard from other Brits competing in America and what I have watched on YouTube, is my main source of knowledge. I apologise in advance for any holes in my knowledge that could have only been remedied by operating in that scene for longer or living in America. I want to celebrate difference and point out ethical distance or problems when I see them.

Before I moved to Edinburgh, I lived in a small town in rural Aberdeenshire called Lumphanan. I went to school with less than five hundred other people and my main exposure to poetry was reading Carol Ann Duffy, Edwin Muir and Shakespeare in English class at school. My nearest poetry 'scene' would have been one or two open mics in Aberdeen city, an hour and a half away by irregular buses. I knew of oral storytelling but had no conception of spoken word or performance poetry. That was until I encountered a YouTube video on a website when I was maybe about sixteen or seventeen. The video was poorly filmed on someone's phone at an obviously American stage. It was immediately recognisable as poetry but still very strange – it was someone speaking loudly, almost yelling at points, over a screaming crowd. I was intrigued.

I don't remember when I first heard the term 'slam poetry' or of a 'poetry slam' but the first one I encountered was during my first week in Edinburgh as a student. There were about two hundred people crammed into a student bar (the Pleasance Cabaret Bar). I was incredibly interested and compelled, and one year later I tried it myself.

I found the unwritten, unspoken rules fascinating. No one ever said directly that these poems had to be the writer's own or that they had to be truthful – yet in my first couple of years I saw people react with obvious confusion when someone read a poem that wasn't their own: whether it be classic e.e. cummings or the modern rapper and poet Watsky. It was as if they didn't really know how to react to someone who was presenting

There's a whole host of performance ethics and it can be overwhelming. Do you have to consider facts about the person who follows you when slamming? Is it unfair to do an angry poem about men and sexism if you're being followed by a man? Or a poem about how students are irritating and lazy if you're at a student slam? There are still so many questions about performance ethics and I don't think this is a negative thing. I compare this to the still forming etiquette around social media. My mother recently asked me if it was okay to delete a colleague from work she didn't really speak to anymore on Facebook. I had to explain to her how this would look pointed with them only having a handful of mutual friends. This reminds me of the forming spoken word scene: is it rude to do a poem based on someone else's? Or one that's part fictional? These answers are still being formed and it is a communal decision of audience, performer, host and organiser.

What looks encouraging is that the rules are becoming less unspoken. In the months after C.U.P.S.I. an American performer I met whilst out there posted in the C.U.P.S.I. 2016 Facebook group encouraging poets to start writing more 'silly' poetry: about happy or random things in their lives. She stated that slam poetry couldn't continue putting its scars and trauma under the spotlight. To me, this is progress. Slams should never get stuck in political or comedy or sad poems being the only ones that win, and with encouragement of these differences, I hope C.U.P.S.I. 2017 flourishes with new styles and happier performers onstage.[33]

---

[32] On revisiting and editing this article several months later, I must add in that some young American poets have started posting on social media about the dangers of performing about trauma. For example, on the 22nd July 2017, user @lutherxhughes tweeted "Dear poets, you don't have to trigger yourself into trauma to get out a good poem. Dear poets, stop telling others to trigger themselves." This received nearly 1,000 retweets and 2,600 likes.

[33] It is also interesting to note that since writing this essay C.U.P.S.I. 2017 took place in Chicago. During the finals there was a feature from Mark Smith, a person many recognise as a founding father of slam poetry in Chicago in the 1980s. The audience members (comprised mainly of poets who had or were competing) objected to his poetry on the basis that it was racist (I was not there and am white, and so can only listen to those who were present). They decided that they would not complete the slam, and that the finals would instead be a showcase of the top four teams. In an address to the audience they spoke about the role of "trauma" in their poetry, and how they disagreed with slams judging trauma and companies like Button Poetry profiting on this trauma. It is unclear what the future of C.U.P.S.I. looks like and whether this will impact the topics writers write and perform about, or the format in which they perform them - but the ethics of slam has certainly evolved to a new and fascinating place.

The Scottish scene has also started adapting. The new Scottish Slam Champion is Daniel Piper, an English poet who has a past in comedy. At the championships he performed upbeat poems on topics from vegetarianism to drugs. His most recent show *Daniel Piper's Day Off* looks at his sheer desperation to get a break from work, with lines like: 'Working from home: the perfect crime!'. In moving from comedy to poetry he shows he's always trying to do something new. Daniel won after only being in the Scottish scene for a couple of months which also signals that the Scottish scene is open to something different and new.

Going forward I can only hope that ethical discussions become more open. At times the total lack of any large infrastructure in the poetry scene is refreshing: it means no limitations and a totally ability to stroll up to a slam, win and go on to perform wherever you please. At the same time, this lack of infrastructure sometimes leaves those who make mistakes without redemption. It can be difficult to know the ins and outs of our assumed ethics and in a community entirely based on word of mouth and who-knows-who, those who make simple mistakes sometimes can be left out in the cold. That is why I believe there should be some way to simply create some kind of adaptable structure, where poets can be forgiven and learn from their mistakes. Instead of silent annoyance at those who flout the rules I hope we either start a discussion with said performer, or question why that specific rule is there to begin with.

9. UNWRITTEN: AN ANECDOTAL HISTORY OF PERFORMANCE POETRY IN SINGAPORE

Ng Yi-Sheng

A Prologue (2010)

It's Thursday night at Blu Jaz Café, a restaurant-cum-lounge bar at 11 Bali Lane, tucked away in the historic district Kampung Glam. We've got a room on the third floor with a chandelier and a sound system and bar service; the writers are huddled near the stage and a girl's been posted at the door to sell tickets. The place is packed to the gills with our audience: they're scanning their menus, ordering chicken fingers and beer and Coca-Cola, but what they're really hungry for is poetry.

A little after 8pm, the slam-master comes on stage: a young Canadian named Arianna Pozzuoli. She warms up the crowd, leading them in "The Singapore Slamthem", introduces the five randomly chosen audience members who'll serve as judges, then kicks off the slam.

Former national champion Marc Nair dishes out his satires of the Orchard Road floods and the Mass Rapid Transit's *Love Your Ride* campaign, while Pooja Nansi reads sensual homages to love from her book, *Stiletto Scars*. Eccentric British expat Alan Ardy chimes in with his sly, erotomaniac rhyming couplets; Ridzal Hamid defies government censorship with "This Is Not a Political Poem"; and Milani, who identifies as an immigrant poet, channels Sandra Cisneros with a paean to her own homeland: "You Bring Out the Indonesian in Me".

After three rounds, the victor turns out to be one of the emerging stars of the scene: the 20-year-old theatre student and former Singapore Idol contestant Benjamin Chow. He wins $75 and the applause of the room. The slam-master invites audience members to sign up to slam next month, and I end up hanging around the bar till well past eleven on this weekday night.

Those are my memories of the *Word Forward Poetry Slam* of 28 October 2010. True, it was a particularly well-attended slam, since it took place after regular slams had been on hiatus for two years. Yet this positive, populist vibe is by no means unusual in the scene that Chris Mooney-Singh and Savinder Kaur have established since their first slam in 2003. A subculture has developed – less mature, perhaps, than what you'll find in many North American, European and Australasian nations – but thriving and provocative nonetheless.

What irks me is that almost nothing has been written about Singapore's slam poetry in academia. In fact, until recently, there's been very little documentation of the history of poetry in performance in our nation, in spite of the fact that many of our most important poets were deeply committed to the performative experience of their works.

I've thus attempted to redress this omission by sketching a brief history of our nation's English language performance poetry scene, focusing primarily on the regular literary readings organised by writing communities over the years. This essay does not trace the parallel narratives of Singapore's Mandarin, Malay and Tamil literary readings. Nor does it dwell on writers who X'Ho, Roger Jenkins and Michael Corbidge, who performed their poetry in the context of theatre and indie music rather than as part of the literary community.

I've also depended largely on interviews for my information. Consequently, major gaps and errors may be present, and descriptions may be coloured by the lenses of subjective memory and personal prejudice. Please write to correct me regarding any aspect of the narrative that misinforms or misleads.

What follows is an imperfect attempt at understanding how performance poetry in Singapore has progressed and regressed over the past 50 years. I can only hope it yields better scholarship from researchers more thorough than I.

Dazzling beginnings: the *Evening of Poetry and Music* (1962-

1979)

There must, of course, have been poetry readings associated with the Straits Chinese literary movements of the 1900s, as well as the proto-nationalist literary movements of the 1950s. Yet if we're talking about a clear, sustained tradition of English language poetry in performance in Singapore, it's probably best to begin with the *Evening of Poetry and Music*, initiated circa 1962 and resumed, after a hiatus, in 1965. Organised by the National University of Singapore (NUS)'s Literary Society, this was the brainchild of two poet-professors, the British chair of the English Department DJ Enright and the then-rookie lecturer Edwin Thumboo—a man who would later be seen as the country's unofficial poet laureate.

Poet and English professor Kirpal Singh attended these readings as a schoolboy in the mid-sixties, and later coordinated them as a university student and young lecturer at their peak in the late sixties and early seventies. They were then held monthly (and for a period of two years, fortnightly), usually at the Upper Quad of the old Bukit Timah Campus, outside the English Department. He recalls the atmosphere of such events:

> 'People would just lie on the grass, and you would find others having a romantic date while listening to poetry and music... It was rubbish to say that people didn't support poetry: there were usually as many as 100 or 80 people on the lawn, and nobody cared if you had a beer can or wine there. In some ways we were less prudish then....
>
> The typical format was that usually at about 6, people would start strolling in. At about 6:15, the MC would start calling people, 'Hello and good evening guys,' and the most staid ones [poets] would read from 6:30 to 7:30. The real music would go on from 8:30 until about 10... The folksy music would come earlier, but the dance disco types came later, when people were really in a smooching mood.'

Besides faculty and student readers, poets from beyond the university were featured. These included Chandran Nair, Sng Boh Khim, Goh Poh Seng and Arthur Yap, who taught at the Regional Languages Centre before NUS. Malaysian poets also appeared on occasion, such as KS Maniam, Kee Thuan Chye and Muhammad Haji Salleh. Australian poets passing through would also come on board, such as Sid Harrax and John Tranter.

It is noteworthy that, after 1965, an almost compulsory policy emerged of featuring representatives from the non-English language poetry scenes. These guest poets included Malay poets SN Masuri, Abdul Ghani, Mohamed Latiff Mohamed, Mandarin poets Chua Chee Lay and Wong Yoon Wah, and Tamil poets Elangovan, TS Iqbal and Ramachandran.

These poets often (but not always) performed their work in combination with music. Such performances might range from simple affairs, such as tinklings of piano keys between stanzas and spontaneous mid-poem guitar riffs. However, Singh recalls more complex forms as well: poems by Thumboo, Robert Yeo and himself were set to choral music by the Singapore Symphony Orchestra; visiting musicians from India dubbed poetry to a drumbeat.

Star musicians were also invited: bands like the Quests and the Bambinos, albeit often minus certain key members; also singers like Susan Lim from Susan Lim and The Crescendos and folk guitarist Robert Liew. Unlike the poets, the bands were often given a token fee for transport expenses, as they sometimes had to hire trucks to bring in their drums. When popular bands performed, audience members tended to congregate on a patch of the green designated as the dance floor.

Singh notes that NUS students were given free admission, though outside visitors paid a small sum. He also remembers the Literary Society's cunning strategy to ensure healthy attendance numbers:

> 'It spread by word of mouth: we always told the boys to get their girlfriends along and got the girls to tell the boys, "If you want to take me to a movie, you'll have to come to the *Evening of Poetry and Music*". So we got boys from Engineering, because they were trying to court our girls; they were from way out at the Dover Campus but they would come to our lawn and indulge. There was a poet called Chung Yee Chong: she used to be hilarious because she was so attractive that everybody would hit on her. There would be some days when more than three guys took her out to the *Evening of Poetry and Music*.

Besides the campus readings, an annual edition of the *Evening of Poetry and Music* would take place at the old Drama Centre at Fort Canning. In such cases, an admission fee was charged for fundraising purposes; and though only about $100 was raised on each occasion, that money could go a long way in those days. Alternative venues were sometimes chosen, such as the National Museum Theatrette, Victoria Theatre and even once the now-demolished National Theatre, which Singh remembers as having rather poor acoustics and technical equipment. A few editions were even held in Malaysia.

'The thing I'm trying to convey', says Singh, 'is that poetry was more than what you saw on the page. The *Evenings of Poetry and Music*, they reached beyond what we would call poems or poetry. They actually made real impacts on people's lives and relationships.'

However, the buzz of the *Evening* was not to last. By the eighties it had become an annual affair, usually held at Lecture Theatre 13 in the new NUS Kent Ridge Campus. Nonetheless, it's survived: it remains a regular event on the NUS calendar today, held in various locations, from the Arts House to the University Culture Centre. It has influenced and been influenced by the movements and communities in the chapters that follow.

An interregnum: the Bistro Toulouse-Lautrec, the Substation, Boat Quay Readings (1980-1996)

In the eighties, a few other notable poetry readings sprang into existence. In 1980, the now-defunct Ministry of Culture began publishing the biannual quadrilingual literary journal Singa; an initiative accompanied by a spattering of *Singa Readings* until 1984.

This was also the decade of the Bistro Toulouse-Lautrec, a French restaurant-cum-blues and poetry bar in Tanglin Shopping Centre. This was a sophisticated spot where fashionable professionals could dine to the melodies of the house band, the African-American jazz singer Cassandra and the Singaporean jazz artist Jeremy Monteiro, or else to the words of prominent poets such as Robert Yeo and Simon Tay, wrangled by entertainment manager Shirley Soh.

The founder, Goh Poh Seng, had been inspired by the performance poetry traditions of Ireland, where he had studied medicine, as well as the Philippines, which he had visited. (In 1977, he famously hired the National Museum Theatrette for the launch of his poetry collection *Lines From Batu Feringghi*, where he spent 90 minutes performing a poem of 3,048 lines.)

Singh notes that some poets at the Bistro would get soused in alcohol before their numbers. Some critics therefore unkindly quipped that the café might better be known as 'too loose, lost track'. Nonetheless, Singh claims that the outlet approximated the decadent atmosphere of a Berlin or Parisian café rather well.

Sadly, this was also a short-lived enterprise. It opened in 1983 and closed shortly before Goh emigrated to Canada in 1986; the readings themselves were monthly for a period of five months, but were ultimately never sustained. Goh left the country disgusted that the authorities had shut down his other bar, Rainbow, because a member of the house band Speedway had uttered a vulgar Hokkien word.

Poetry readings gained momentum again in the nineties. The founding of the Substation by playwright-director Kuo Pao Kun in 1990 was a crucial moment, as it provided an independent multidisciplinary arts space for emerging writers. Regular readings, often accompanied by music, were held in its garden, with a peak period from 1994 to 1996, though stretching on to the anti-Iraq War rally of 2003.

Meanwhile, Tope 'Sky' Omoniyi, an energetic young Nigerian poet-professor, had begun teaching English at the National Institute of Education (NIE). From 1995 to 1996, he organised a series of monthly readings in Boat Quay, where performing poets were treated to a jug of beer as payment for their services.

A few of these readings were particularly memorable as they were held on board a bumboat. Yong Shu Hoong was a featured poet at one of these evenings afloat, and he remembers them as informal, intimate affairs, with audiences of just 20 to 30 people, sipping wine. 'The nice thing about it was that it was open-air, and if the weather was good you could see the sun setting on Singapore River', he says. On the downside, acoustics were often pretty poor.

But Omoniyi knew he couldn't run his readings forever. His teaching contract was due to expire in 1997. To ensure some form of succession, he called for a meeting at his NIE office with four poets: the Chinese-American lecturer Chin Woon Ping, the Singaporean computer programmer Yong Shu Hoong, a local teacher trainee named Alvin Pang, and a Singapore Tourism Board employee named Paul Tan. Red-eyed with emotion, he pleaded with them to take on his mantle. Little did he realise how well they'd answer his call.

Rebirth of the word: the *Forum Readings, Art Aloud, Afterwords* (1997-2000)

The poets of Singapore didn't start just one monthly reading in 1997 – they started three. The first, in February, was a continuation of the Boat Quay readings, which Omoniyi's four protégés rebranded as the *Forum Readings*.

The premiere edition of the *Forum Readings* took place in the chapel of the newly refurbished CHIJMES, a former convent now transformed into a lifestyle hub. Later sessions were mostly in the second-floor gallery space of Caldwell House, the former living quarters of the nuns, or else in the gazebo area. Tan eventually assumed leadership of the event, assisted by Yong and fellow poet Heng Siok Tian.

In spite of the glory of the performance space, it had its shortcomings. 'They [the readings] were a bit clinical, because really, the venue was too grand to be an intimate setting', says Pang, who was frequently in attendance. 'Audiences were small, the space was echoey. You had to try very hard to fill that space with presence, and that was not easy at all'.

Pang thus decided to break off and start his own monthly reading series, partnering with his fellow York University alumnus Aaron Lee. Late in '97, they began *AfterWords*, held at the recently opened Borders megastore in Orchard Road. This was more of a loungey, talk-shop event than a reading per se, and thus had a more populist attraction for the audience.

The third set of readings that began that year was *Art Aloud*: a monthly open mic at the Singapore Art Museum's Olio Dome bistro. Initiated by SAM itself, the sessions were often hosted by the curators of the *Forum* and Borders readings: Pang, Lee, Tan, Yong and the like.

This crowded literary calendar caused some headaches. The organisers would try to coordinate amongst themselves so that each of the three readings would take place during a different week of the month, for fear that they'd begin cannibalizing each other's writers and audiences.

There were also legal worries. According to the writ of the law, all arts events in Singapore had to be licensed by the Media Development Authority, including innocuous literary readings. The application process for each reading could've taken over two months and would've left little room for impromptu numbers.

'I was pretty gung ho and I said, "We'll worry about it when we worry about it,"' says Pang. 'I refused to get a licence, but I know some people wanted to for theirs, or [they wanted] CHIJMES to get a blanket licence. I remember one of the discussions where one of the co-organisers said we wouldn't proceed unless we got some kind of blanket licence.' Fortunately, the poets never ran into any trouble – not even following risky incidents, such as when Pang's poetry open mics at SAM were hijacked by the activist James Gomez with his political tracts, or by the playwright Elangovan intent on performing the entirety of his banned play *Talaq*.

In fact, the government-sponsored Singapore Writers Festival continued to hire Pang et al to host readings and panels and open mics at the Substation and the National Library. Pang believes this early decision set the precedent for today, when most literary event organisers wouldn't dream of applying for a reading licence (although some, including myself, have been pressured by the MDA into doing so).

Over the years, the territory changed. In '98, the *Forum Readings* moved to the old National Library Building at Stamford Road, where performers read their works al fresco in the courtyard by the art deco fountain. Then, in '99, Pang ended *AfterWords*, discouraged by a change in the bookstore's management. A burnt out Paul Tan ended the *Forum Readings* in 2000.

> 'It was all very exhausting. And I think in hindsight, it was too much too soon. But that's how ecologies grow: you have to let everything grow at once', says Pang. He notes that the Internet may have had something to do with the die-off: now writers had the chance to express themselves on on-line journals, forums, billboards and blogs, there was no longer so much of a pent-up need to share poetry via performance.'

He notes a further factor: 'Every mother's son's brother was publishing poetry and doing a reading at the launch'. Publishers like Landmark and Ethos Books were issuing volumes by Alfian Sa'at, Felix Cheong, Gwee Li Sui, Toh Hsien Min and the like. *AfterWords* and the *Forum Readings* had established the value of performance as a marketing strategy at launches. Combined with other one-off events, the literary famine wasn't too extreme.

Before the slam: *subTEXT* (2001-2008)

Oddly enough, the two years preceding the first slam in Singapore proved to be crucial for Singapore's performance poetry tradition. According to Alvin Pang, it was in those lean years that he and his compatriots learned the genuine skills of how to present poetry on stage.

'To me, 2001 was quite a landmark, because that was when we started touring [the multi-poet anthology] *No Other City*,' he says. 'The influence was two-way. [Firstly,] because we had to go out there and show our work, we had to step up our delivery. Secondly, we saw what other people did. In Australia, we were very much exposed to what performance poetry is all about, so we started adopting performance styles to make our poems work on stage.'

Pang would continue to develop his skills the following year, when he received an invitation to the Austin International Poetry Festival with his fellow poets Grace Chia and Toh Hsien Min. The three of them resolved to prepare for the event by undergoing basic theatre training under actor Sim Pern Yau. In a complimentary one-day workshop, Sim communicated the basics of movement skills, based on a philosophy of inner mastery – a lesson that's stuck with the poets since. (Sim has since retired from acting to become a full-time tai qi master.)

Meanwhile, the scene in Singapore wasn't lying completely dormant. Paul Tan had urged Yong Shu Hoong, one of Sky Omoniyi's original protégés, to continue the tradition of hosting literary readings. The result of this was *subTEXT*, first held in May 2001 at the lounge of the Gallery Evason Hotel. This monthly reading series would prove to have stamina, and would endure over the next seven years.

subTEXT would later move from the hotel to the Books Café on the second level of the old MPH Bookstore on Stamford Road. This eatery was burdened by a noisy coffee machine and an absence of mics, yet it's fondly remembered for how it provided poets with complimentary gourmet tapas and canapés: chips with salsa and pesto chicken dips, easily worth fifteen dollars at today's restaurant prices.

The reading's third and final location was the new National Library Building in Bugis. Here, readings were housed in the basement's Multi-Purpose Room – a rather sterile space, but furnished with technical equipment. Writers occasionally had their texts projected on screen as they read, and even (in my own case) exhibited YouTube videos based on poems.

It's impossible to give a representative list of featured readers at *subTEXT*, as it would include pretty much everybody active in writing in Singapore in the 2000s. Guests ranged from newly published poets like Teng Qian Xi to indie songwriters like Typewriter's Yee Chang Kang to renowned foreign authors such as Alexander McCall-Smith and Paul Theroux. (Theroux's reading was held in the Pod, a room shaped like a flattened globe on top of the National Library. It commanded a record audience of 200. As the Pod was only designed to hold 150 people, Yong was worried at the time that it might fall off the top of the library.)

Even today, long after its January 2008 dissolution, *subTEXT* still lingered on. Yong continued to hold the event on extremely ad hoc basis, with the last edition to date in 2012, and used his email list to keep his base of bibliophiles in the know about nationwide literary events.

Slam emerges: *Word Forward* (2002-2003)

Yet *subTEXT* didn't impress everyone. A recent immigrant to Singapore attended in 2002 and found the general level of performance inhibited – none of the poets had memorized their work beforehand, and seemed mostly content to simply sit down and read their three poems in undramatic voices.

This spectator was, of course, the future founder of Singapore's slam scene, Chris Mooney-Singh. Born Chris Mooney in Canberra in 1956, he'd studied journalism at Mitchell College of Advanced Education, with an additional major in creative writing. During this period, he organised poetry readings on campus and created poetry programmes for the local student radio station. Upon graduation, he began publishing in poetry journals across ANZAC, and also became the poetry editor for an environmentalist magazine in Perth named *Simply Living*. Here he printed the likes of Les Murray, Judith Wright and other established Australian poets.

'I started performing myself during the early '80s,' he recalls. 'There was a kind of strong push, a lot of energy in the Australian poetry scene at that time. The Sydney poets, the Melbourne poets and the Canberra poets, and the other cities' poets all kind of tussled with each other. [There was] good energy and the necessary locking of horns that happened in poetry scenes and literary scenes.'

Mooney moved to Adelaide in the mid-eighties, home of *Friendly Street Poets*, the longest running community open mic in the southern hemisphere, alive and well since 1975. Here, he began to practise performance poetry in earnest, experimenting with music, even founding a poetry performance ensemble in 1991.

But as nourishing as the Adelaide scene was, he chose to spend most of the nineties traveling around India, researching oral traditions of poetry. It was here that he converted to Sikhism, inspired by the centrality of the

Granth's sacred poetry to the faith. While in New Delhi, he produced a poetry and music fusion CD, called *Indian City*.

In 1997, he toured the Sikh gurdwaras of Singapore and Malaysia, attempting to promote his CD. During his stay, he performed at the Substation and attended a poetry reading at Zouk Club. More importantly, he met Savinder Kaur, a Singaporean corporate trainer who would become his wife just two years later. The two of them went on to work in India, researching sacred Sikh music and working to revive the rabab, a medieval string instrument that had fallen out of fashion over the last 400 years.

Then in July 2002, the couple migrated back to Singapore. Mooney-Singh was intent on returning to his roots in performance poetry: after all, he'd hosted poetry readings and created poetry radio programs as a student and had participated in the vibrant performance culture of Adelaide's Friendly Street Poets gatherings.

His first step was to found *Four Crying Out Loud*, a poetry performance collective. The quartet originally comprised Mooney-Singh, *subTEXT* host Yong Shu Hoong, American writer Richard Lord and Singaporean poet and contratenor Cyril Wong – though Wong left after their first showing at the National Library, and was soon replaced by the painter-poet Julyan Perry. Performances were created using mostly original works, and were tailored to fit a seasonal theme. For instance, the Deepavali/Halloween performance at the Substation was titled *Shadows and Voices: Light and Darkness*. Perry, now mostly forgotten in the world of poetry, proved to be quite the performer: 'He's got a gift for accents. He could do Adolf Hitler rhetoric and he could do Irish pirate ballads,' Mooney-Singh says.

Thanks to this work, Mooney-Singh was invited by the National Arts Council to serve on a working committee for the Singapore Writers Festival 2003. The idea emerged of holding a domestic poetry slam event. He was thus given funding to attend the Austin International Poetry Festival to investigate – but first, he began e-mail correspondence with Marc Kelly Smith, the man generally credited as the founder of slam poetry.

'He let me stay with him in Chicago and introduced me to the leading North American slam poets,' he recalls. 'The National Body for Poetry Slam [probably the committee of Poetry Slam, Inc.] was also meeting up, so I actually met everybody of note: the people who've had almost 20 years of history in poetry slam and who were already the elders of slam tribe. They had their ups and downs but they were still very community-centered, very poetry-centered, all about an art form generated by poets for a public. I traveled around for about a month, went to many poetry slams in different states, and recommended that Marc be invited to come to Singapore for that Festival.'

Mooney-Singh didn't stop at the recommendation, though: he was inspired. He made an agreement with Zouk Club to begin his own regular performance poetry event. He founded *Word Forward* as a company, and in May 2003, he kicked off Singapore's very first poetry slam. This was held at Velvet Underground, a lounge bar owned by Zouk, decorated with Keith Haring and Takashi Murakami prints.

Controversially, he also registered 'poetry slam' as a trademark, so that no other group in Singapore could hold an event with such a title without his company's permission. This decision was made based on the advice of the American slammers, who warned against the devaluation of slam culture by amateur groups.

'When Chris came back [from the US], he told us that he saw that slam was the new wave and the thing that was going to save poetry and reinvigorate poetry in Singapore and the many other cities', says Richard Lord. As a veteran of the Boston spoken word scene, he became deeply involved in these early slams, usually performing opening numbers as part of *Four Crying Out Loud.*

'I can remember that early on, the slam was very well-attended', he continues. 'Zouk was packed, every slam. It was sort of an in-thing: you had a number of Mediacorp celebrities who would show up. I remember one time there was a little group of artistes including [fashion model] Nadya Hutagalung.'

The slam's greatest moment of glory came just a few months later, on 23 August at the Singapore Writers Festival. The bar was packed to the point of ridiculousness, mostly because of the fame of the guest star, Marc Smith himself, who kicked off the night with his own dynamic mixture of original and cover poetry.

Although it was officially a National Arts Council event, Mooney-Singh feels he can take credit for the evening's triumph. 'We had actually warmed up the scene considerably before [Marc Smith] got here, he says. '[NAC] rode on the model we had already created. They held it at our own venue, at Zouk. They followed our procedure. A lot of new people came to the slam through the Writers Festival, naturally, but I don't think it would have had the impact if slam had not been launched four months earlier.'

Indeed, considering the newness of slam, Singapore poets acquitted themselves rather well in the competition. Some, such as then-NUS student Marc Nair, were gallantly testing out pieces they'd written for the page rather than the stage; others like radio DJ Greta Georges displayed obviously honed skills in half-sung, half-spoken delivery. Plus, there were so many competitors that results had to be released after only two rounds: it was getting past the NAC officials' bedtimes.

This was a landmark in our literary history – and also an event of personal significance to myself. After all, it was the first slam I competed in, and one of the very few I won.

Slam rises, slam falls: the Zouk years (2003-2008)

Slam continued to prosper at Velvet Underground for the next few years. I was able to observe this from a front-row seat. Although I was still finishing my university studies in New York, I came back at the end of almost every semester to compete and spectate.

The slams were held, as they still are now, on Thursday nights at 8pm. Often, they would be set to a theme: a love slam around Valentine's Day, a haiku slam, an all-women's slam, even experimental slams using Mandarin, Tamil and pantuns. Guest artists were varied; they included poets, singers, non-fiction writers, theatre-makers and film directors. Velvet accommodated the tech demands for this easily – it not only boasted a large projection screen, but also several smaller monitors so that we could survey the action from the bar area.

Mooney-Singh often kicked off the competitive portion of the night with a self-composed anthem, "The Word Must Rock", which explained the rules of the game. This was when the slammers came up: a surprisingly diverse group of people drawn from both the expatriate and local communities. Besides Georges and Nair, there was Alan Ardy, with his flamboyant dress sense, carnal love couplets and Asian girlfriend on his arm. There was Hari Kumar, an awkward computer programmer from India whose poems were often sweet family anecdotes rather than diatribes. There was Bani Haykal, a National Serviceman whose surreal verbal compositions reflected his background as a songwriter for the indie rock group B-Quartet. And there was Pooja Nansi, a university student whose work reflected her tumultuous romantic past and her Gujarati immigrant roots.

Though I'd hesitate to claim that a specifically Singaporean style of slam emerged, others have noted that our mainstream is quite distinct from the hip-hop-influenced variety that's become prevalent in the United States. Poems tend to be less explicitly political, less angry, with greater variation in format. 'We're still a little bit rojak [a Singaporean English term meaning 'mixed up'], a little bit all over the place, and I like it', says Nair. 'It's more personal. You hear the poet more than the form'.

A few published poets were slam participants as well, including Felix Cheong, Robert Yeo and Yong Shu Hoong. Even the established playwright Stella Kon took a stab at it. But by and large, there was little intermingling between the two worlds. Established writers, including myself, weren't used to the casual cruelty of the amateur judges, who had little patience for abstruse or poorly performed work. Mooney-Singh claims that pride was involved: 'A lot of people declined because they didn't want to be associated with this lower form of poetic output. For some, we've been seen as a kind of opposition to the 'government of poetry' in Singapore in some way.' Alvin Pang has a different story: he says he stopped going because he couldn't see what the fuss was about – he'd seen much better slams abroad.

Ultimately, Nair emerged as one of the slam's most frequent champions – thanks in no small part to Mooney-Singh. 'Chris is really my mentor, helping me to develop my own poems', he says. 'He would look at my work and go down to the level of real language: "You need to like develop more striking imagery", or "Cut the feminine end rhymes". We'd also talk about the poem, the emotions behind it. Sometimes I'd have the idea but it wasn't fully formed, so I'd discuss it with him'.

It soon became apparent that his work was worthy of publication – as was the work of a number of other committed slammers in the group. Thus, at the Singapore Writers Festival 2007, Word Forward launched four self-published poetry collections: Mooney-Singh's *The Laughing Buddha Cab Company*, Nair's *Along the Yellow Line*, Pooja Nansi's *Stiletto Scars* and Bani Haykal's *Sit Quietly In the Flood*. These last three writers have since been recognised as Singapore's first generation of native slammers.

The same year, *Word Forward* successfully planted the seeds of slam in Kuala Lumpur. The city has since developed a thriving spoken word culture, supported by key players such as Elaine Foster, Sheena Baharuddin,

Jamal Raslan and Jerome Kugan. (Not all such initiatives have gone as planned, though: despite a promising event at the Man Hong Kong International Literary Festival 2004, slam has yet to take root in that region.)

Yet times had changed in Singapore. Slam audiences were clearly dwindling – on numerous instances, I recall we had to endure freezing temperatures in Velvet Underground, caused by a combination of hyperactive air-conditioning and sparse body heat. Poets stopped coming, either because of a change of interest or a change of address. Several, including Georges and Kumar, had left the country to pursue work in other lands. Richard Lord recalls the dramatic change in atmosphere:

> 'The love poetry slams had been one of the best attended and ardently competed of the slams. I think they had to refuse people the right to compete simply because they already had twelve people signed up. A couple of times people were pissed off because they didn't arrive early enough [to sign up].

> But a few years later, we had a love poetry slam and it was very well publicized. And at the end, Marc Nair and I were going to be the only two competitors, and we didn't have enough people to be judges [in the crowd]. We were going around just begging people who'd stumbled into Zouk to compete, and in the end that evening we didn't have a slam - we all just sat around and read cover poems which Chris and Savinder had brought along. I think that was the last slam I ever went to at Zouk.'

There were several reasons why Velvet Underground wasn't an ideal location – the large size of the space, the mandatory entry charge of ten dollars and the pillars which blocked most audience members' view of the stage. Perhaps the biggest issue, however, was Zouk's reputation as a liquor-soaked club for adults – something the parents of young poets didn't quite approve of.

Given all these problems, it was no huge surprise when *Word Forward* ceased its slams at this venue, shortly after its fifth anniversary in 2008. 'At that point I suppose we felt we needed more new voices that were not coming through', Mooney-Singh reflects. 'So we felt the need for a bit of a rest: to clean out the well and let new water fill up'.

In January 2009, an attempt was made to rise from slumber. Discussions were carried out with Literati, the literary society of Singapore

Management University, to make their annual slam a monthly event. However, this fell flat due to a lack of sustained support from students. Our nation's high-pressure education system, alas, does not stimulate the development of literary communities.

Slam and education (2004-2009)

While things looked gloomy to former audience members of Zouk, insiders at *Word Forward* knew the situation was more complex. The monthly slam was by no means the only activity they were invested in: what was far more important was the business of poetry as education.

As early as 2004, Mooney-Singh and Kaur had managed to score a regular source of funding from Creative Communities Singapore, a division of the Ministry of Community, Youth and Sports aimed at arts outreach. One of their first moves was to send out a letter to every junior college and secondary school they could contact, offering to conduct free poetry workshops. Similar workshops were later initiated with university students, thus attracting writers like Nansi and Ridzal Hamid to the slam.

With her background in corporate training, Savinder Kaur became a key player in this area of *Word Forward*'s work. She built up a strong administrative framework for performance poetry education in schools, including detailed curricula and lesson plans. Today, the company is regularly invited to schools to present performance poetry assembly shows as well as workshops – a program which gives Ms Kaur an opportunity to actually pay young slam poets to teach and perform their poetry.

According to Mooney-Singh, 'Poetry slam has answered a strong need to give a voice and a platform to young Singaporeans to help them overcome their self-consciousness in public speaking. Young people are much more open to exploring poetry and presentation and performance, and actually poetry slam had to find new poets, new audiences'.

Kaur adds: 'When Chris brought in poetry slam, I realized this is a powerful tool to bring into the classroom. So many things can be learnt. That's the power of poetry'. She's particularly triumphant about the company's successes at the Institute of Technical Education (ITE), traditionally seen as the dumping ground for the lowest-scoring students in each cohort. 'ITE people cannot believe that their students can appreciate poetry. But one girl, she talked about her family problems onstage and she cried, and all the facilitators were shaken. I'm very proud that poetry slam has served this way'.

Through collaboration with the British Council, *Word Forward* has also been able to bring in some rather renowned mentors from the UK for their workshops: poets like Malika Booker, Charlie Dark and Jacob Sam-La Rose. Mooney-Singh was also individually responsible for engaging pioneer American slammer Ray McNiece, who worked with the company in Singapore for over six months.

According to Mooney-Singh and Kaur, Sam-La Rose was especially impressed by one of the company's interschool initiatives: the National Youth Poetry Slam League (NYPSL), first set up in 2005. This event allowed teams and individuals from schools across the nation to compete for a slam title, watched by an audience of thousands. Inspired, Sam-La Rose went on to develop similar nationwide events for the UK, including the Apples & Snakes Word Cup and Shake the Dust – the country's largest national youth slam to date.

Since 2006, the NYPSL has been incorporated into the National School Literature Festival, a day-long event featuring performances, debates and parades, held in a different school each year. This in turn gave rise to the launch of Lit Up in 2009, an annual literary festival aimed at youth and emerging writers, usually lasting two weeks. Both Singaporean and international writers were involved, with some guests coming from as far as Kenya and Botswana. A National Poetry Slam League for non-students was also incorporated into the festival, with a special incentive for the winner: he or she would go on to represent Singapore at the Réunion Island Poetry Slam, a contest for poets from across Asia and Africa.

Marc Nair was the first to claim this prize in 2009. Looking back, he confesses he was highly intimidated by the African slammers' revolutionary anthems, and more than a little disoriented when, as a half-Malayalee, half-Chinese Singapore citizen, he was asked to do a poem in his native language. (In the end, he opted to read in Malay, which he had studied as a second language in school.) Nonetheless, he ultimately managed to place third in the whole competition, and went on to compete at the Poetry Slam World Cup in Paris.

An Indie Renaissance (2010-present)

With the inception of the *Word Forward Poetry Slam* at Blu Jaz Café, regular slams have returned to Singapore after two years' absence. The new venue served them well: the location's central, the space is intimate without being insanely cramped, enough drinks are served to keep the adults happy, and enough food is on the menu to reassure parents that it's a restaurant instead of a vice den. The company still charges ten dollars per head, but it saves money on advertising, thanks to the zero-cost medium of Facebook invites. The only drawback, really, is that poems are occasionally drowned out by the indie music blasting downstairs.

And as hoped, new voices have broken through. There's Deborah Emmanuel, who commands the stage with her stirring confessional pieces; Nabilah Husna, who takes on social issues with sardonic humour; Stephanie Dogfoot, who brings a queer feminist activist voice to the table; Jennifer Champion, whose eccentric observations of city life are mixed with deep soulfulness; Shivram Gopinath, who skewers anti-Indian racism with his wit, and Charlene Shepherdson, who's developed a foolproof system of improvisational poetry. Also Benjamin Chow, Lee Jing Yan, Goh Koon Hui, Abel Koh, Zuni Chong, Amber Lim, Kok Wei Liang, and many, many more.

Meanwhile, the first generation of slammers has matured: each one is now creating projects that extend far beyond the three-round structure of slam. Nair has published eight further collections of poetry, including *Chai: Travel Poems, Postal Code, Animal City* and *This Is Not a Safety Barrier.* He's served as the frontman for his band Neon and Wonder, and co-founded *Mackerel,* an online culture magazine. Pooja Nansi has mastered the guitar and does shows fusing bluesy poetry and music, and has published a second collection, *Love is an Empty Barstool.* In 2017, the Poetry Festival (Singapore) appointed her as their first Youth Poetry Ambassador. As for Bani Haykal, he's gained close to mainstream fame, first with *B-Quartet,* then with the renowned band *The Observatory.* He's also founded the multi-disciplinary art collective mux, performed solo shows at the Substation and the Esplanade, frequently designs sound for theatre productions, and has been featured as an artist in the Singapore Biennale. Notably, all three poets have been conferred the government's Young Artist Award.

It'd be natural to assume all these developments are part of Chris Mooney-Singh's plans to build up the Singapore spoken word scene. Yet the truth is, he was absent from Singapore from 2010 to 2015, as he was completing his PhD studies at Monash University. In his absence, young slam poets began to reclaim the scene for themselves, integrating it with the country's emergent indie arts culture.

From 2012 to 2015, Marc Nair worked at *Word Forward* as the Artistic Director of Lit Up. He transformed it from an event for student writers into a broader indie arts festival, featuring not just spoken word but also rap battles, band gigs, gallery exhibitions, performance art, literary workshops, black box dramas and comedy improv.

A major highlight of the festival was its annual collaborative spoken word project. In 2011, fifteen writers, actors, artists, musicians, photographers and origami practitioners came together to create *The City Limits*, an inter-disciplinary performance on urban Singapore, staged at the newly opened Goodman Arts Centre. In 2012, a spoken word troupe was formed called The Party Action People, with eight poets performing solos and choral pieces in the soon-to-be-demolished Telok Ayer Performing Arts Centre, where *Word Forward*'s office had been housed for years. Collaboration went international in 2013, with *She Walks Like a Free Country*, an all-female spoken word revue, highlighting injustice, repression and patriarchy in Singapore and Malaysia. From Kuala Lumpur, we had Elaine Foster, Sheena Baharuddin and Melizarani Selvakkumar, bringing down the house with Jennifer Champion, Victoria Lim, Nabilah Husna and Raksha Mahtani. This took place at at Aliwal Arts Centre, where *Word Forward*'s new office was housed.

Beyond the purview of the company, a wave of regular, independently organised spoken word events arose. I was part of this movement myself: from March 2011 to January 2015, I recruited spoken word artists for *SPORE Art Salon*, a multidisciplinary evening of visual and performing arts initiated by American choreographer Ryan Beck, principally organised by photographer Olivia Kwok, and hosted by ECHO Loft, then Blu Jaz Café, then Artistry Café.

In June 2012 *Destination: INK* emerged: a monthly open mic series, where poets, prose writers, musicians and other artists have a safe space to showcase their work. Held at Blu Jaz, it's the brainchild of spacer.gif, a collective set up by writers Charlene Shepherdson, Nabilah Husna and Vanessa Victoria. From January 2013 to November 2016, Home Club played host to the open mic platform *SPEAK*, organised by Deborah Emmanuel, Vanessa Victoria and Stephanie Dogfoot. One of their biggest coups was hosting American spoken word sensations Sarah Kay and Phil Kaye, who performed in April 2013 to a fully packed club. Then in May 2013, Pooja Nansi started *Speakeasy*, a literary program at Artistry, each edition focusing on one or two major poets or collectives from Singapore or abroad. Besides the familiar faces of the slam community, they've showcased Alvin Pang, Cyril Wong, Alfian Sa'at, the women's arts group *Etiquette*, George Szirtes from the UK and TJ Dema from Botswana.

Readings and recitals continue outside the circles of poetry slam. The independent bookstore BooksActually has been the host of innumerable literary events since its opening in 2005, including Poet X Poet, Babette's Feast and variegated book launches. The Arts House has remade itself as a centre for a higher class of literary events, such as *World Voices*, which showcases non-Singaporean writers, and Yong Shu Hoong's *New Word Order* series of talks and readings. These institutions have been remarkably inclusive towards spoken word artists: in fact, the first two NUS-Arts House Poets in Residence for 2012 and 2013 were British performance poets, namely Jay Bernard and Jasmine Cooray.

One of Singapore's newest and most vigorous literary initiatives, *Sing Lit Station*, grew out of this fertile environment for poetry. In April 2014, Pooja Nansi and Joshua Ip started Singapore Poetry Writing Month (*SingPoWriMo*): a Facebook-based campaign challenging people to write poems for every day of April. This event culminated in a reading at BooksActually and an anthology launched at the Singapore Writers Festival that year. The campaign subsequently became an annual affair, drawing thousands of contributors and spawning many more projects, including a few memorable poetry readings held in carriages of the MRT (Singapore's subway system) and the upper deck of a bus.

In July 2016, Ip formally unified these projects under a non-profit organisation called *Sing Lit Station*, which holds workshops, writing residencies, manuscript boot camps for poets and novelists. Notably, its online database of Singaporean poetry, poetry.sg, places young spoken word poets on the same footing as the established page poets of yesteryear. It's even commissioned a historical anthology of Singaporean spoken word poems, tentatively titled *Unwritten Verse* and edited by Marc Nair, Pooja Nansi and myself.

With so many new avenues for emerging writers to share their work, it's arguable that the influence of *Word Forward* has somewhat faded. It still holds the National Poetry Slam League: following Nair's success, the victors have been Stephanie Dogfoot (2010), Lee Jing Yan (2011), Nair again (2012), Victoria Lim (2013) and Shivram Gopinath (2014 and 2015). Yet it's had to put the event on hold for 2016 and 2017, and it no longer has international links. The Réunion Island Poetry Slam has shut down due to lack of funds.

Stephanie Chan was Singapore's last international representative in 2010. Surprisingly, in 2013 she went on to compete at the Poetry Slam World Cup in Paris – on behalf of the UK, where she was based as a student.

Epilogue: Slam futures

Chris Mooney-Singh still harbours big dreams of developing an Asian Slam League, covering the Anglophone regions of India, the Philippines, Malaysia and Hong Kong as well as Singapore.

This would give poets the means to build careers, he claims. 'In America, the reason why the poetry slam scene has worked out so well is because they've created a network, a performance circuit. So, people travel to North America and on to Europe, earning their full-time living from poetry – maybe very modestly, but they do it. They can do it because poetry slams are spread out, and visiting poets have somewhere to perform next week, and they keep traveling'.

He adds: 'Once you have regular [events]: weekly, monthly and annual events, national events, people will get better. With more stages, more opportunities to create their art and craft and they become more professional at it. Without creating a continuing circuit for this, poetry slam can wilt a bit, because you're basically performing with the same audience, just like a singer needs to keep moving to new gigs'.

As of now, Singapore's already developed a rudimentary circuit for poets. This was evident in August 2013, when a team of visiting Burmese poets were able to play three venues on three successive nights: BooksActually on Monday 12th, *World Voices* at The Arts House on Tuesday 13th, and *Speakeasy* at Artistry Café on Wednesday 14th – an impressively packed calendar.

Yet it's too soon to say if this new poetry-loving climate will last. Tracing the history of performance poetry here, one notices how quickly readings are snuffed out and forgotten, how there's an ebb and flow to the culture of literature in performance. One major problem we're facing is high rentals: to ensure a profit margin, cafes, bars and clubs often pressure organisers of readings to charge more for admission, leading to a breakdown in their relationship.

What will change in the coming years? Can *Word Forward*, or another literary organiser, set up an international network of spoken word events, fostering the cross-pollination of our literatures? How will this affect the literature and culture of Singapore, and of other nations?

These questions shall serve as a subject of study for future academics and members of the literary community. For now, the answers remain tantalisingly unwritten.

10. SPOKEN WORD AS A WAY OF DISMANTLING BARRIERS AND CREATING SPACE FOR HEALING

Emma Lee

Leicester, in the UK, has a vibrant spoken word scene which supports and gives space to many voices, among them those who are not normally heard or who would find printed word environments intimidating. The city's spoken word scene encourages inclusivity and breaks down barriers, thus enabling poets who have experienced trauma to work towards healing in a supportive environment.

People who have been through trauma need two things (once physical and medical needs have been addressed): validation and acknowledgement.[34] They need to know their feelings in response to the traumatic event(s) are valid and acknowledgement that the traumatic event(s) happened but should not have done. Seeking validation and acknowledgement is not easy. Traumatised people are often shamed or feel that they are partly to blame - especially if they are victims of domestic or childhood abuse and/or sexual assault - and attempts to talk about their experiences are met with denial or attempts to blame the victim for the abuser's actions. Some victims may feel that their voice is merely one of many and play down their experiences because they feel they are better off than others, for

---

[34] Robin H. Gurwitch, Anne K. Messenbaugh, *Healing After Trauma Skills: A Manual for Professionals, Teachers, and Families Working with Children After Trauma/Disaster*, http://bit.ly/2qSapEx

example, survivors of a major incident or accident, refugees fleeing war, a group of citizens who have been systematically discriminated against and disadvantaged. South Africa's Truth and Reconciliation Hearings were an important way of acknowledging Apartheid was wrong and validating the experiences of Black South Africans.[35] There were fears the Hearings would stall progress towards unification or would produce overwhelming data that would not cohere into useful information, but these underestimated or ignored the value of acknowledgement and validation to the victims.

Poetry is turned to at times of extreme emotion, such as poems read at funerals or written/sung to celebrate love. Poetry's brevity, structure and texture gives it a perfect framework in which to explore feelings and experiences the writer is struggling to articulate, which would sprawl, expand, loosen and deviate without bringing clarity in prose. Poetry pushes writers to strip ideas down, to focus on what they are saying and how they are saying it. It is as much about the space around the poem's words as it is about the words. Poetic devices such as metaphors or analogies offer a way of exploring and expressing a subject without being explicit. Both traditional forms and free verse offer a way of bringing some order to disorganised, disorientated thinking.[36]

Currently there aren't any poetry magazines based in Leicester city, so, for city-based poets, sending out poems for publication means sending them to an editor the poet has never met. Even when poets know their poems are of publishable standard, the world of publishing is still predominantly middle class, white and male, so rejections don't come as a surprise. Further rejections encourage the suspicion that it's not the poems that are at fault, and that the rejections are more about the poet not fitting in. For some poets, the more rejections they get, the harder it becomes to keep submitting poems for possible publication. Standard rejection slips don't usually give a reason for rejection and don't usually encourage a submitter to try again. The combination of seeing poems in print that don't look like the poems a poet is writing and standard rejection slips is

---

[35] Truth and Reconciliation Committee South Africa, http://bit.ly/2qUoxxa
[36] Matthew Lieberman, "The Brain's Braking System", *Neuroleadership* http://bit.ly/2qSvjnh

discouraging.

With spoken word evenings, poets gain admittance just by turning up. Everyone gets an equal time slot and a round of applause. There's generally no special treatment for regulars or established poets. Attendees have an equal opportunity for feedback. Asking someone to have a more in-depth look at a poem is easier and some spoken word events encourage attendees to speak to poets to get feedback.

Leicester's longest running spoken word night, *Word!*[37], provides a welcome to all poets, from beginners to established poets. Its main organisers, Lydia Towsey and Tim Sayers, also work in mental health settings. However, none of the attendees are forced to label themselves. Poets are introduced by name only and the poet decides how to introduce their poems. It is the poet's decision as to whether they say their poem is based directly on personal experience or whether they wish to identify as part of a group that frequently suffers discrimination. This is important because it puts the poet in control and places the focus on the poem. Labelling the poet takes attention away from the poem and risks putting the poet in a ghetto. For example, not labelling the poet, stops X from being known as a poet who only writes poems about mental health issues or Y as a poet who only writes about the experience of being from an ethnic minority in the UK. Not labelling the poet also gives the poet space to grow and develop in other ways. There is applause after each poem and people reading at Word! for the first time get a round of applause too. To sign up for the open mic slots, poets must arrive an hour early, which offers a chance for attendees to mingle and discuss poems heard at previous events, poems in progress and writing poems. In addition to *Word!*, Leicester offers *Shindig*, organised by Nine Arches Press and Crystal Clear Creators; *House of Verse*; *Anerki*; *Pinng...k*; *Find the Right Words*; the *Peoples Arts Collective*; the *Rhetoric Literary Society*, who focus on teenagers and younger people; and Leicester City Libraries' *Write On*, a Leicester Writers' Showcase with performance space at the central library once a month.

Too often, even well-intentioned people, can exacerbate trauma by

---

[37] Word! http://bit.ly/WordLeicester

putting words into a victim's mouth or expecting a victim to behave according to prejudices formed by an observer. Being unable to speak or being silenced by vocalised or implicit denial or victim-blaming, causes harm through lack of validation and acknowledgement. Being able to speak offers control and ownership. Speaking to a supportive listener, whether that's one trusted person or a supportive community through poetry, creates opportunities for acknowledgement and validation to take place.

Leicester has a tradition of welcoming refugees and is one of the most ethnically diverse cities in the UK with no overall ethnic majority. No one ethnic group makes up 51% or more of the population. The 2011 census showed that 45% of Leicester's residents are white British and 49% of residents are from Asian, African, Caribbean or mixed-race backgrounds.[38] This diversity is reflected at spoken word events where people from non-white ethnic backgrounds feel more confident of a welcome than if they submitted work to poetry magazines.

When the current refugee crisis hit the headlines in 2015 and, emboldened by politicians, including the then Prime Minister David Cameron, the right wing press felt able to use divisive language about refugees.[39] The idea for *Over Land, Over Sea: poems for those seeking refuge* was born.[40] It rose from the need to give voice to the alarm that was shared among poets at the suffering and hardship people who are seeking refuge were, and still are, experiencing. It started in August 2015 with a Facebook group bringing together the publisher, co-editors and supporters.[41] Two of the co-editors, Siobhan Logan and I, are Leicester-based poets. The third co-editor, Kathleen Bell, lives in Nottinghamshire and works in Leicester, teaching Creative Writing at De Montfort University. Kathleen Bell's 2014 pamphlet, *at the memory exchange,* was shortlisted for the Saboteur Awards. Siobhan Logan has published two collections with Original Plus and led

---

[38] Leicester City Council's paper following 2011 Census, http://bit.ly/2qULRe7
[39] David Cameron criticised for language used to describe migrants, http://bbc.in/2qSQ55Y
[40] *Over Land, Over Sea: poems for those seeking refuge,* edited by Kathleen Bell, Emma Lee and Siobhan Logan (Five Leaves, 2015).
[41] Poets in Solidarity Facebook Group, http://bit.ly/2qT4tLP

Writing East Midlands' first ever digital writing agency in 2014. All three of us regularly attend poetry and spoken word nights in Leicester, and Siobhan Logan and I are members of Leicester Writers' Club. The publisher, Five Leaves, is based in Nottingham where owner Ross Bradshaw owns a bookshop of the same name. A call for submissions was issued on 2 September 2015.

One of the aims of *Over Land, Over Sea: poems for those seeking refuge* was to raise funds for charities working with refugees. In total 204 poems were submitted from Europe, Iraq, USA and Australia. Due to practicalities and time pressures the anthology only included poems in English, a language common to all three co-editors. Despite the anthology being monolingual, the support was still tremendous. Some contributors expressed relief at being given an opportunity to provide a counter-narrative to the one offered by the media by being able to write and talk about how they felt about what was happening and a chance to show solidarity with people seeking refuge. The anthology enabled poetry to become active: it made connections and empowered poets to write, speak and raise funds to help others. It helped poets, who were vicariously traumatised by events they were witnessing, realise they could do something.

Over Land, Over Sea: poems for those seeking refuge was published on 1 December 2015. There were similar initiatives, Eyewear's *Refugees Welcome: Poems in a Time of Crisis* which was published later in December 2015; Marie Lightman's *Writers for Calais Refugees* blog, which sought to raise awareness of refugees' plight was set up on 30 August 2015; and various Poem-A-Thons in 2016, where poets were sponsored to read poems to raise funds. One Brighton-based Poem-A-Thon has raised over £30000 for charities.[42]

To begin with *Over Land, Over Sea: poems for those seeking refuge* was a print publication. Subsequently readings were held in Leicester; Nottingham; at the StAnza Poetry Festival at St Andrews in Scotland and at the Poetry Cafe in London. Some of those readings were at the invitation of Leicester's Human Rights Arts and Film Festival, the

---

[42] *Refugees Welcome: Poems in a Time of Crisis*, edited by Oliver Jones (Eyewear, 2015); Writers for Calais Refugees, http://bit.ly/2qTxEhF; Brighton Poem-a-thon http://bit.ly/2s52vbv

Leicester Migration Network at Leicester University and London-based Exiled Writers Ink. The readings, and Facebook group, offered contributors the chance to meet each other and build a sense of community. Since publication, there has been a Journeys Poems Pop-up Library where postcards featuring poems from the anthology were handed out to travellers at Leicester Railway Station; two contributors read poems at the *Day of Sanctuary* at the Houses of Parliament in London[43] and these were followed by *Journeys in Translation*.[44]

It was acknowledged that a disadvantage of the original anthology was that it was monolingual. *Journeys in Translation* therefore encourages poets and translators to translate the poems into other languages and organise readings of the original English poems alongside translations with discussions around the difficulties in translating poems either from English or into English. *Journeys in Translation* is not restricted to fluent bi- or multi-lingual poets and translators, but includes people who are learning a language or have some language skills they are not confident in so that they can develop those skills and gain confidence. For example, one participant has translated some of the poems into her mother tongue, Arabic, and now feels more confident using English. One *Journeys in Translation* session, run in conjunction with a refugee charity, encouraged those who were learning English to pick phrases from the poems they recognised and translate them into another language. It has also provoked discussions around cultural translations. For example, one poem uses space as a metaphor for the alienation and othering of refugees. This caused difficulties for one poet attempting to translate the poem into Shona because there was no direct translation for some of the astronomical terms. The focus of *Journeys in Translation* is to enable people to speak, to own their stories and develop language skills so they can resist being spoken for and can control what is said about them.

Ingrid de Kok's "Parts of Speech" asks if the stories behind dry courtroom records can become 'rhymes that start in the heart' and 'verbs that move mountains'.[45] The question assumes that readers are

---

[43] Sanctuary in Parliament, http://bit.ly/2qUMbtl and http://bit.ly/2qSWyhw
[44] Journeys in Translation, http://bit.ly/2qVKX14

passive and that there is no interaction between writer and reader. That is often true of printed words that lie flat on the page and rely on a reader's interpretation coinciding with the author's intention. At a spoken word event, the audience need not be passive. The audience can hear the poet read their own words, telling their story precisely as they need it to be told. The audience can hear tone, rhythm, and emphasis, and see the poet's expression. There may be an opportunity to ask for clarification. There is also opportunity for the audience to share their own stories when it is their turn to read, even after a gap of several weeks. Leicester's spoken word scene encourages poets to make these connections by creating a supportive environment. In doing so, the scene makes it possible to enable poets who have experienced trauma to work towards healing.

---

[45] "Parts of Speech" is from Ingrid de Kok's *Seasonal Fires: New and selected poems* (Seven Stories Press: New York, 2006).

11. THE BURNING BUSH:
A CASE STUDY OF (PERSECUTED) POETS IN
SAUDI ARABIA, IRAN, AND JORDAN

Madiha Bataineh

A Saudi poet of Palestinian origin, Ashraf Fayadh was a curator within Saudi Arabia's art scene as well as a blogger working with the British-Arabian arts organization Edge of Arabia when he was sentenced to death for apostasy, convicted, among many things, of having spread atheism through poetry. Among his 'disputed' poems were those published in his collection *Instructions Within*, first published by the Beirut-based Dar Al-Farabi in 2008 and later banned from distribution in Saudi Arabia.[46] Within this collection were poems like "A Melancholy Made of Dough", "On the Virtues of Oil over Blood", and "The Last of the Line of Refugee Descendants", all which offer a critical and creative look into aspects of Saudi society, its complexities, and problematics. Several poems from *Instructions Within*, as well as Twitter posts and coffee conversations were among the evidence used against him in Saudi's court of law. In an article for *The Guardian*, Middle East researcher for Human Rights Watch Adam Coogle stated that the poet's death sentence reflected the Kingdom's 'complete intolerance of anyone who may not share government-mandated religious, political and social views'.[47]

Fayadh's disputed poems are laments, not cryptic or coded but bold and provocative. Among the themes he tackles are religion, economic

---

[46] "New Translated: Poems to Read for Ashraf Fayadh on January 14", *Arab Lit*, 11 January 2016, http://bit.ly/AshrafPoems
[47] David Batty, "Saudi Court Sentences Poet to Death for Renouncing Islam", *The Guardian*, 20 November 2015, http://bit.ly/AshrafSentence

inequality, and the social hypocrisy of the Saudi State. The poet criticizes the corruption and greed integral to Saudi Arabia's oil business. 'Petroleum is harmless', he writes in "On the Virtues of Oil over Blood", 'except for the trace of poverty it leaves behind'.[48] Fayadh treads on several contentious grounds, operating his creative pen on a national landscape known for its censorship and silencing of the arts in light of its economic, social, and political policies. Indeed, Saudi Arabia was ranked third in a list of 'The 10 Most Censored Countries' by the Committee to Protect Journalists.[49] The report affirms that since the Arab Spring, Saudi has 'progressively intensified legal repression', and applied legal mechanisms that have 'punished the publication of any materials deemed to contravene sharia, impinge on state interests', among other 'violations' which, it seems, have come to include poetry.[50] Fayadh extended his opprobrium to confront the economic problematics of the world's second largest oil producer, Saudi's intensive capitalism and materialism, and the social hypocrisy of the land.

While Fayadh's poetry, written in Arabic, was initially published exclusively through his blog, following the incident and his imprisonment, discussions and translations of his work spread through digital platforms. In the same month as his sentence (November 2015) the *Berlin International Literary Festival* published a petition to support the writer with a Worldwide Reading on January 14, 2016, which prompted the reading of Fayadh's work in many languages (including French, Spanish, Finnish, and Turkish), and in over 40 countries around the world. As the case gathered global attention, Fayadh became an iconic figure and honored as an Honorary Member by German PEN.[51]

The poet's story and work reveal the constraints operating on creativity and expression in Saudi Arabia, where a government has long regulated the boundaries of art by rule of Shari'a law. Fayadh was unafraid to tackle controversial topics regarding Saudi Arabian restrictions and regulations on freedoms. Among these poetic protests, he writes: 'He's got no right to walk however, or swing however or to cry however, he's got no right to open the window of his soul, to renew his air, his waste, and his tears', commenting on the lack of freedom that starts from his physical

---

[48] Ashraf Fayadh, "On the Virtues of Oil Over Blood", translated by Mona Zaki, *Arab Lit*, 14 January 2016, http://bit.ly/OiloverBlood.
[49] "10 Most Censored Countries", *Committee to Protect Journalists* (2015), http://bit.ly/CPJ2015
[50] Ibid.
[51] "New Translated: Poems to Read for Ashraf Fayadh on January 14", *Arab Lit*, 11 January 2016, http://bit.ly/AshrafPoems

existence and extends to opening 'the window of his soul', the deeper and complex aspects of his being.[52] In February 2016, Carles Torner, Executive Director at PEN International argued that Fayadh was sentenced to death 'simply for exercising his legitimate right to freedom of expression' and as such, insisted 'we will continue to press the Saudi authorities for his immediate release'.[53] In a translation of Fayadh's poems on grief and imprisonment on World Poetry Day by the Guardian, the poet lamented: 'Freedom is *very* relative: all said and done we live in a ball-shaped prison barred with ozone'.[54]

Most contentiously, Fayadh dared to confront the religious boundaries held with the highest reverence in Saudi society. Alluding to his skepticism against religion, Fayadh writes 'of intersecting with your obscene withdrawal from that flabby religion from that fake *Tanzeel* from gods that had lost their pride'. Fayadh dared to challenge religion in a state that regards it as supreme, to call it and the 'tanzeel' or given law, 'flabby' and 'fake', in addition to later writing that the 'prophets have gone into retirement, so don't expect any prophet to be sent your way for your sake', reminding his readers 'you have put your soul at the hands of those who do not know much', suggesting that it is not religion that he criticizes but those who have hijacked it for their own ends.[55]

In his poem "The Last of the Line of Refugee Descendents", among his most renowned, Fayadh wrote: 'You give the world indigestion, and some other problems', and it is in fact this gift of 'indigestion', his own in regard to the society he inhabits and the need to process and share it through poetry which he offers his online followers.[56] In the same poem, he writes: 'A new formula has been developed to eliminate recalcitrant dirt, And at only half the price. Hurry to buy up half the amount.' Here, he refers to the formula of persecution, the silencing of the poet's voice, which reaches beyond the normative boundaries of Saudi's material, political or religious oppression; a landscape operating under the pretense of ethical doctrine but in reality, furthering unchecked political, economic, and social control. Fayadh reminds his readers that the prophets have done into

---

[52] Ashraf Fayadh, "Ashraf Fayadh's 'Disputed' Poems, in English Translation", translated by Mona Kareem, 23 November 2015, http://bit.ly/2qZ69mY
[53] "Reduced Sentence & Flogging for Poet, Ashraf Fayadh, Wholly Unacceptable." *PEN International*, 2 February 2016, http://bit.ly/AshrafPEN
[54] Ibid.
[55] "Worldwide Reading of Selected Poems and Other Texts in Support of Ashraf Fayadh" *Worldwide Reading*, 14 January 2016, http://bit.ly/2qWLa3V
[56] Ashraf Fayadh, "The Last of the Line of Refugee Descendants", translated by Jonathan Wright, *Arab Lit*, 11 January 2016, http://bit.ly/2qXSKvr

retirement; they are no longer present, or even relevant, in the State's implementations.

In a public letter and show of solidarity published by PEN and signed by many poets around the world including Carol Ann Duffy, Paul Muldoon and Adonis, writers protested:

> 'We, poets from around the world, are appalled that the Saudi Arabian authorities have sentenced Palestinian poet Ashraf Fayadh to death for apostasy…It is not a crime to hold an idea, however unpopular, nor is it a crime to express opinion peacefully. Every individual has the freedom to believe or not believe. Freedom of conscience is an essential human freedom.'[57]

Following the international outcry organized by PEN and ArabLit and thousands of writers around the world who participated in the World Reading, Fayadh's case went 'viral'. With this strong support, his death sentence was reduced in February 2016 to eight years in prison, eight hundred lashes, and a repentance via social media.[58] A seemingly anachronistic struggle reminiscent of the 18th century, the episode reflects Saudi Arabia's use of religion to enforce a contemporary intolerance towards contentious subjects of expression, showcasing an ugly reality: the modern Arab poet has been flogged and imprisoned in the pits of Saudi prison. In a public statement, Fayadh has said: 'People should know I am not against anyone here, I am an artist and I am just looking for my freedom'.[59]

Though Fayadh remains in prison, the poet was lucky to have received the support of the international community, which took on his cause, annulled his death verdict, reduced his sentence and gave him hope as a writer when his words were heard—but Irani poet Payam Feyli was not so lucky when it came to international support following his censorship. Indeed, the gay poet faced a similar battle when he was blacklisted and detained by Iran's morality militia for his words but all his attempts to respond or gather a global campaign for support failed.[60]

Growing up in a 'post-Islamic Revolution mullah-run illiberal

---

[57] Alison Flood, "Fellow Poets Protest Saudi Death Sentence Facing Ashraf Fayadh", *The Guardian*, 27 November 2015, http://bit.ly/2qXYWTU
[58] "Reduced Sentence & Flogging for Poet", ibid.
[59] Ibid.
[60] Joshua Yasmeh, "Gay Poet Persecuted in Iran Looks for New Home in Israel", *Daily Wire*, 3 March 2016, http://bit.ly/2qXyxFY

theocracy' where clerics have operated as civic administrators to propagate puritanical Shite religious 'morality' and institute homosexuality as a cardinal sin and capital offense punishable by death or flogging, life as a gay man was a struggle for Feyli.[61] In defiance of Iran's authoritarian regime, he began writing about his orientation from an early age, making no attempt to hide it in writing. His book *I Will Grow, I Will Bear Fruit...Figs* starts with the bold sentence: 'I am twenty one. I am a homosexual. I like the afternoon sun'.[62] Fencing his sexual preference between his age and fondness for the afternoon sun, Feyli placed his sexuality, one of many element of his identity, on equal footing with the other aspects of his self. Soon after the book's publication, Feyli was blindfolded in a shipping container at an unknown location for 44 days.[63] Failing to gather enough support for his case, the writer was eventually forced into exile, ironically landing on enemy soil in Tel Aviv, where a liberal community welcomed his work and allowed him to publish poetry and stage plays that openly expressed his sexual identity and life story.[64] Feyli spent a decade resisting Iran's religious frontier before moving to the 'promised land'.

Feyli was arrested for the first (out three) time in 2011 and was detained for nearly a month. In 2014, he was again arrested, this time for 44 days: 'He was at home alone when three bearded men forced their way into his house, wrapped him in tape, blindfolded him, and brought him to a garden where he was kept in a shipping container'.[65] These actions set boundaries on the creative output, assuming creative inflexibility in the context of Iran's illiberal and despotic precedents. They hijacked and imposed chosen standards of 'morality', driving it as a political and social boundary arbitrarily defined by a group of religious fanatics. Feyli was blacklisted and sought foreign publishers to publish his work, eventually succeeding to publish eight books abroad.[66]

At fifteen, Feyli started writing poetry and at nineteen, in 2005, he published his first collection (in Persian) *The Sun's Platform*. This was the only one of his works to be released in Iran, and even then it was only circulated for two years before the Ministry of Culture and Islamic

---

[61] Ibid

[62] Payam Feyli, *I Will Grow, I Will Bear Fruit...Figs: Man Sabz Mishavam, Miveh Midaham...Anjir* (UK: H&S Media Ltd, 2011).

[63] Joshua Yasmeh, ibid.

[64] Ibid.

[65] Nina Strochlic, "Iranian Poet Blacklisted for Being Gay", *The Daily Beast*, 3 July 2014. http://bit.ly/PayamExile

[66] Ibid.

Guidance expulsed two long poems they found to carry 'political and anti-religious undertones' and immediately placed his name on the list of 'banned authors', blocking him from publishing in Iran again. [67] In 2010, he published *I Will Grow…* the story narrated by a homosexual boy. 'It was like introducing me to myself', Feyli said of working on the novel. 'By writing this story I created an image of my life and through that image I could get to know myself'.[68]

The theme of his homosexuality continued as a thread throughout his work and poetry, and penalties began accumulating in his life: from being fired from his job as an editor at a publishing house to his social media accounts being hacked (presumably by the government), the authorities worked to ensure that Feyli would not find platforms or local support to showcase his work. 'After that, anybody I wanted to work with inside Iran, they would go to him, threaten him, and stop the work between us', he stated in his interview with the *Daily Beast*. His friends were receiving the same visits and lost touch with him out of fear.[69] Feyli was cast out of society.

Having been prevented from garnering a local audience through institutional or traditional routes in Iran, Feyli attempted to reach out for a global audience and launched his digital campaign, "Publish Payam & Outsmart the Censor #IamPayam," to raise funds, publish, and translate into English his collection of love poems *White Field*, in which Feyli 'grieves for Iran's imprisoned activists, a deceased lover, and creatively expresses his own internal battles'. According to the website, contributions were said to help 'translate, edit and print the poetry *White Fields* in English', 'Create the digital edition of the book'. 'Publicize the book and get it into the hands of every literature lover across the world who supports freedom of speech and is against censorship and discrimination', and 'take a stand against Iran's censors'.[70] The "I am Payam" campaign emphasized: 'with no regard for content or style, the censors have completely blacklisted [Feyli's] works'. The campaigners hoped to make Feyli's case global, 'help us to get Payam's voice to the world', they wrote—but it failed.[71] Unlike with Fayadh's international outcry, the campaign failed to reach its funding goal, collecting only five hundred pounds of the seven-thousand-pound objective.

Meanwhile, attacks on Feyli continued, threats amounted, and articles

---

[67] Ibid.
[68] Ibid.
[69] Ibid.
[70] Ibid.
[71] Ibid.

were published about Feyli in the Iranian media, describing him as a homosexual, a traitor, and a Zionist collaborator to overthrow the regime. The poet continued to suffer; his health went downhill as a result of this ostracizing and he fell into a depression that checked him into a mental hospital. In response to these events, Payam wrote:

> 'I grieve for my morning paper, vilified
> I grieve for my books, bowdlerized'[72]

Now working on his seventh book of poetry called *The Sad Whales*, Feyli had to turn to exile in order to continue writing his story and fight for his words, but only one of his poems, published in the *Missing Slate* has been translated into English. Still, he maintains hope regarding his poetry, saying:

> 'Because I come from a country where the government is
> always talking about wars and hatred, as an author I want
> my message to other countries and readers to be a
> message of peace'.[73]

Meanwhile, Iran's censors are ensuring the poet's words do not filter back into his country.

Unlike Fayadh, who garnered global support to change the course of his story and have his work reach a global audience through translations, Feyli failed to garner sufficient attention and was obliged to leave his home country of Iran to continue his literary and creative career. While the two poets' cases collected different momentums, one succeeding in influencing the outcome of the case (though he is still serving an eight-year prison sentence for writing poetry) and the other driving the poet to exile, both share the fate of the persecuted poet writing within the context of restrictive regimes operating under the jurisdiction of Shari'a law. Both reflect the poet's struggle and longing to express and critically analyze the status quo of the land he inhabits. Both have acted as the 'voice of the burning bush'.

In both these cases, the Saudi Arabian and Iranian regimes outlined their intolerance for controversial themes emanating from poetry. Jordan, also a country legally operating under Shari'a law, however, has remained a more liberal context for freedom of expression in the region, especially when it comes to poetry. Indeed, among the few writers actively seeking to

---

[72] Payam Feili, "Eleven", *The Missing Slate*, 24 December 2013, http://bit.ly/11missingslate
[73] Nina Strochlic, ibid.

stir these grounds was poetry slam champion Aysha El Shamayleh, an Ivy-League educated and self-published poet who, in the seven years since returning to Jordan after getting her Bachelor's Degree from the University of Pennsylvania in Economics, Political Science, and Philosophy, worked through creative, educational and entrepreneurial endeavors to encourage poetic expression in Jordan. She directed initiatives like the USAID-funded Takamol Gender Programme to get youth engaged in creative expression and critical examination of social and gender boundaries. A *Jordan Times* headline published in December 2015 following the culmination of the initiative's first round read 'Poetry slam gives young people a voice on social issues'.[74] In 2015, El Shamayleh co-founded Writers Cell, a Middle Eastern startup dedicated to innovating and producing creative content for a young intellectual audience in the Arab world. But prior to these initiatives was El Shamayleh's realization that opportunities for poets were scarce in the kingdom.

After winning the 2007 and 2008 National Collegiate Poetry Slam Championships in the US and featuring on the cast of Russell Simmons' 2009 documentary *Brave New Voices* which aired on HBO, El Shamayleh started performing her poetry at local venues to bring Slam Poetry, or Spoken Word Poetry to Jordan. El Shamayleh believed in the power of performing poetry rather than simply publishing, and she was bold and unapologetic when she brought her poetry back to Jordan. In her poem "Political Footnote to the Arab Poet", for example, clearly influenced by the style of Beat generation, El Shamayleh delivers a daring affront to the ever-present reality of bloodshed and hypocrisy in the Middle East:

'You want to know all the details, what got the poet to fall
into dark rooms mothering mics, thick wire, and electric?
… I was born a traitor in August of 1988, that summer saw
the Middle East dancing in a lethal red dress in an endless
seduction with war…'[75]

She took a poetic strike against the politics, history, injustice, and 'complicit system', and offered a daring performance of her poetry to over one hundred people at Jordan's first funded and quality independent arts showcase and music venue, *BalaFeesh*. The showcase had recognized the poet's talent and the country's lack of alternative creative platforms, and

---

[74] Dana El Emam, "Poetry Slam Gives Young People a Voice on Social Issues," *Jordan Times*, 10 December 2015, http://bit.ly/2mtoIe3

[75] Balafeesh. "Aysha El-Shamayleh - Political Footnote to the Arab Poet (ft. Shirin Kamal)" YouTube video, 21 November 2014, http://bit.ly/2msW5xH

invited El Shamayleh to share her art and critical yet creative performance:

'I was never given a full, or new, or quarter of an identity,
I was simply lied to
Hey lies, I was taught that kings aren't peacocks

Hey truth, the schools cared more
about the color of our shoes than walking us to you

The schools worried about the consequences of using the
word whore in a sentence but never bothered to stop the
bullying that walked the tender souls into nooses!'[76]

In an interview, El Shamayleh insists her journey as a spoken-word poet in Jordan was limited because the audience is small and publishing opportunities are non-existent.[77] Indeed, her independent career as poet was short-lived and she began carving new molds for younger generations to find what she had not. Furthermore, with the lack of publishing houses promising both quality and marketing opportunities in Jordan, El Shamayleh refuses to trust her work into the hands of local publishers and insists, 'If I get published, I'd want to publish abroad'. Yet back in 2015, El Shamayleh self-published her poetry collection *Anatomy of Fire* to accompany her showcase at *Balafeesh*, but the collection did not propagate beyond the stage and she remains largely unknown, though her recorded performance at *Balafeesh* garnered some attention on YouTube and other online platforms.[78]

El Shamayleh insists that there is a growing desire for writers 'to be relevant in the world that [we] live in', especially in a country like Jordan where censorship has focused in the opposite direction of the case studies in Saudi and Arabia; working to mute religious extremism rather than enforce it. Nevertheless, the country harbors a weakness in both the production of quality and bold creative content, and its propagation, and as El Shamayleh says, 'the writer is the weakest link in the Arab world'.[79]

With Jordanian universities and English departments across the kingdom promoting curriculums without a creative writing component, and the study of English or language at universities reserved for those who score the lowest grades in High School, it is no surprise that a culture of

---

[76] Ibid.
[77] Madiha Bataineh, Interview with Aysha El Shamayleh. 1 June 2016.
[78] Aysha El Shamayleh, *Anatomy of Fire* (Amman, Jordan: Self-Published, 2014).
[79] Bataineh, ibid.

12. "OUR BRAINS HAVE CHANGED, NOW THERE ARE PLACES IN OUR MEMORIES THAT ARE EMPTY": IN CONVERSATION WITH MARTÍN RANGEL

Interviewed by Claire Trévien
Translated by Lawrence Schimel

Claire Trévien: You are a published poet but also a performer – how do the two co-exist for you?

Martín Rangel: I think that the traditional methods through which poetry reaches people (reading sitting behind a table, the academic scene) only function in a seat of what for me represents a complete poetic experience. When you bring poetry to the stage, through visual or audio supports (which are not so different, I would call them instead: elements), through the very corporeality of the poem and of the poet as the speaker, the full poetic experience becomes increasingly less a utopia.

It is difficult to live between both worlds. It is difficult to want to do something in one place that you can't, and vice versa. Sometimes, in the most conservative spaces (and this is not news), it is not possible to completely unfurl the reaches of the poetic. And I try to take it all with a dose of humor.

You've just come back from the Guadalajara Book Fair, what were your highlights?

Luna Miguel reading "Museum of Cancers". Alicia lying on the bed reading a manga by Ito. My friend and maestro Jorge F. Hernández, my beloved Pedro Serrano. My friends, the lovely city itself, my debt with the bank for having bought so many books…

Do you feel part of a particular spoken word scene in Mexico? How would you describe it?

I feel part of a scene that I understand as the freest one in terms of what you can do. Sometimes there are these crews in which you just can't rap, or others in which you can't just recite or project a poem, visually. In Bala Fría, my crew, you can do all that. I can only talk about what I know. My crew and I, we organize monthly open mics called *Nadie quiere escuchar tus poemas (No one wants to hear your poems)*, and people really open themselves there. It's also very crowded. I would describe it as: open.

Has spoken word always been a big part of Mexican culture, or would you say it has recently grown?

It has grown, I feel, since the generation of Rojo Córdova (et al) started doing their thing. Like ten and something years ago, maybe? Recently, according to what we've experienced with Bala Frías's events, I can tell you it has gown a lot. It's a big thing now. I believe I can even say: spoken poetry is bigger in terms of offer-demand than written poetry.

There's some debate about memorising poetry in the UK – do you perform poetry off by heart or do you hold text in some form, or a mixture of both? What are your feelings on this?

I would love to recite my poems by heart but my memory always betrays me, haha. So, I usually help myself with my phone. I keep it handy. I recite and then I forget what I was saying or vice versa, then I look at the document on the phone and that's how I know what's next. I believe it is just evolution, you feel me. Our brains have changed, now there are places in our memories that are empty. Places that used to be inhabited by maps, phone numbers, bank accounts, deadlines, almost everything. Almost. I believe we are adapting to this.

YouTube and other social media are becoming more and more intertwined with spoken word – how do you feel about these blurred lines between digital and physical spaces?

There is no line. As Vicente Monroy say's 'virtual reality is also reality'. Whether the poetic instant occurs in a digital platform or it happens live, the edict doesn't vary that much. However, the virtual experiences give you chances that a simple body-to-audience experience would be unable to display. Unless you had the right gear of course, and that's expensive.

Which performances of poetry has haunted you to this day and why?

There's two, or four. One by this guy Adam Gottlieb called "Poet breathe now". The other one was a video piece by Julian Herbert called "2 poemas para baños". The most recent ones have been, Martha Mega and César Bringas in person. And virtually: Horacio Warpola and Canek Zapata. Carolina Villanueva. What they've been doing.

If you could change anything about your local spoken word scene, what would it be?

I'll invent one. LOL.

Who are your favourite poets?

I have many favorite poets. I like Eduardo Lizalde and I like Bonifaz Nuño, I like Jorge Eduardo Eielson and I like Jesús Arellano and I like Ulises Carrión. I like Kate Tempest. I like Symborska and I love Anne Sexton. I like Nathy Peluso. I like Paola Llamas Dincro, Esther M. García. I love Alicia Ter-Veen, I really like Mira Gonzalez, Jiseland and Luna Miguel.

I've encountered your work through Lawrence Schimel's translation of it – can you tell me about the process of that collaboration?

Lawrence and I met for the second time during a translation residence in Banff, Alberta, Canada, in June of 2017. The first time took place in Madrid in the summer of 2015, I don't remember it because I was very drunk or simply because I'm forgetful. Hahaha. We became friends again easily. He understands me in many things. Very 'majo' [nice] as he'd say. It's difficult to separate yourself from someone you meet in hell. Even worse for someone you meet in paradise.

You've written a poem about translating poetry, with one line saying 'I translate to steal / and I let myself be translated to be stolen'. How do you choose who to translate – and do you have a favourite experience of translation?

I choose to translate the poet who hits the lowest blows. It seems to me that I say so in the poem: I translate the poems that makes me feel, after reading them, 'holy fuck, *why didn't I write that poem?*
But I can no longer write it, because someone else has already done so. Then I translate it. In that way I write it again. And I learn some things, that's always good. That is the only way in which I've translated until now.

If you had to describe the state of spoken word today in Mexico – how would you?

Growing. It is growing. And it will continue to grow. Into ramifications that I might not like at all. The same way that what we do now is uncomfortable for people who are used to sleeping at poetry readings. Not anymore.
Poetry is important. It has a place in our culture. It helps us to exist. But we need make people acknowledge that. That's the hardest thing. And the best part.

13. THE SHROPSHIRE LITERARY SCENE

Rachel Buchanan

'In the comely land of Teme and Lugg and Clent and Clee and Wyre'

I cursed my dear friends as I stumbled over this line from John Masefield's *London Town* in preparation for reading at their wedding in Shropshire last autumn. The poem describes the poet's love for the landscape of the area, the rivers and hills that surround us, and how London just cannot compare. He's right that the land is beautiful, wild and rolling and scattered with sheep and forests, with the Welsh mountains to the west and a line of medieval fortified towns and castles marching from south to north.

This former Poet Laureate's description of Shropshire, even though he hailed from neighbouring Herefordshire, does make a change from AE Housman, the only poet ever really mentioned in relation to the forgotten county where I grew up, his *Shropshire Lad*'s 'blue remembered hills' printed over anything that stands still long enough in gift shops, tea towels, coasters, signs, notebooks and more. You'd think that no other writers ever existed or wrote about the region, but a little digging around and it is possible to find more than a couple of Shropshire writers that people have actually heard of, including playwright John Milton, who wrote *Comus* about Ludlow Castle, our most famous son Charles Darwin, the poet Wilfred Owen and fiction writers Barbara Pym and PD James, who lived in Ludlow briefly before going to university in Cambridge. Most of them didn't, however, write particularly about Shropshire, unlike mid-20th century writers Mary Webb, whose rural novels such as *Gone to Earth* and *Precious Bane* were parodied in *Cold Comfort Farm*, and is kindly described as a romantic novelist, and Malcolm Saville, whose cheerful *Lone Pine Club* children's novels inspired more than one family holiday to the region. Both are largely forgotten these days, but still have devoted and lively societies devoted to promoting their work. Saville's novels were recently adapted into a play and toured by local theatre company Pentabus, leading to a small but definite surge in sales as new audiences, including me, discovered him.

More recent novels about Shropshire include the *Cadfael* series by Ellis Peters, set in Shrewsbury, and Phil Rickman's series about an exorcist detective, Merrily Watkins, such as *The Smile of a Ghost*, set in Ludlow. Also writing now we have Kate Innes, who has had recent success with her medieval drama *The Errant Hours*, Manda Scott, who began life as a crime writer, but these days writes about Boudica and the Romans, Katy Moran, who writes YA fiction about the Dark Ages amongst other topics, and Kate Long, whose novels such as the *Bad Mother's Handbook* only distract from her vole-spotting hobby. What binds all these writers together, as I look at them in this list, is their fascination with history and nature, two qualities with which Shropshire abounds. There is something about the landscape surrounding you that seeps into your bones, someone said to me recently. Local non-fiction writers also clearly take a lot from their wild surroundings, with two of my favourite books of the last few years both written by Shropshire authors: Katherine Swift who writes about rehabilitating an old garden near Bridgnorth in *The Morville Hours*, and *Dip*, by Andrew Fusek Peters, in his memoir describing wild swimming throughout the year. Beautiful writers, all, and well worth a read if you haven't already.

But what of the live literary scene in Shropshire at the moment? People aren't just quietly writing long books in their cottages, they are also sharing writing with each other in a scene that, for a sparsely populated area, could be considered quite lively. Wenlock Poetry Festival, organized by Anna Dreda of Wenlock Books has been an annual fixture since 2010 and attracts world-class poets with a line-up that is never less than excellent.[83] The last time I went, Carol Ann Duffy was holding packed out audiences spellbound in a local school auditorium, and other names on the programme lists include Simon Armitage, Daljit Nagra, Luke Wright and

---

[83] Wenlock Poetry Festival, http://bit.ly/WenlockPoetry

Gillian Clarke. When she's not running the festival, Anna runs themed monthly *Poetry Breakfasts* in the café down the road from her shop, with a strict 'published poems only' meaning that quality is assured, and egos are not bruised... unless, like me, you hadn't read the rules and taken along a poem of your own making, in which case, the freshly baked croissants are at least a consolation for the lack of participation. She has also recently expanded her event list to include *Knitting and Poetry* evenings (these could have been designed with me in mind!), with wine and cake and readings in her cosy shop after hours.

Further north, the Shrewsbury Festival of Literature ran for the first time in November 2016 and included performances by John Agard and Louise Doughty, amongst others.[84] Shrewsbury also boasts poetry groups that meet regularly to share poetry and support such as *Shrewsbury Poetry Stanza*[85] whose member Robert Harper's new literary periodical *Bare Fiction* raised enough money through crowd-funding and subscriptions to begin to spread its wings as far as stockists in Cardiff and London, and was runner up for a Saboteur Award in 2015. Regular reader and organizer Liz Lefroy just won the Café Writers Poetry Competition organized by the Poetry Society, and curates her evenings to include both local and invited poets. At the poetry night I went to, the standard was mostly pretty high, with a mix of traditional poets and one younger spoken word artist who divided the crowd somewhat with his more informal style but proves that spoken word has even reached the Marches. The atmosphere was supportive, and the night is proving so popular that it has now grown out of its first coffee shop venue and moved to a larger room in town. Both writers are part of the new wave of poets in Shropshire who have studied poetry at postgraduate level in recent years, Harper in Manchester and Lefroy at Keele, and have come back home with new energy and a need to keep that poetry candle burning, even in the depths of the countryside.

Another Keele graduate is Deborah Alma, the *Emergency Poet*, with her act in a vintage ambulance that she courageously drives up and down the country to festivals and events. Supported originally by a small Arts Council grant, the *Emergency Poet* act could be described as a sweet and inspired one-woman immersive performance experience based on a simple

---

[84] Shrewsbury Festival of Literature, http://bit.ly/ShrewsburyLit
[85] Shrewsbury Stanza, http://bit.ly/ShrewsburyStanza

premise: let Deb prescribe you poetry for your ailments. I found my appointment to be a really moving experience, involving sitting in the ambulance with a red blanket tucked around my knees, answering Deb's questions and then being offered a poem, complete with directions about how and when to read it, from her file at the end. Deb's assistant, Nurse Verse, curates the outside waiting room, complete with poetry books, poemcetemol (tiny capsules filled with mini poems) and more. The *Emergency Poet* has proved a massive hit, and I last saw Deb parked outside Southmead Hospital in Bristol as part of their festival of health and wellbeing, offering her poems to doctors and patients alike. She has since launched two poetry anthologies, including her latest, *The Everyday Poet,* as well as her own collection of poems *The Tales of the Countryside* published by the fantastic Birmingham-based Emma Press.

A couple of years ago, Deborah Alma and her friend and fellow poet Jean Atkin set up the *Ludlow Poetry Lounge,* running every other month above the Blue Boar pub in town[86]. Jean is another of the poetry scene's energisers, and, as well as running writing workshops in woodlands and schools and performing poetry herself, she has also been Poet in Residence at nearby Acton Scott Historic Working Farm Museum, and was one of Writing West Midlands' supported Room 204 writers. Featuring invited guests as well as an open mic, the evening is usually stuffed full of regulars, and the highlight so far for me was the night that John Hegley came to read, finishing the evening with a rousing version of 'Guillemot!' complete with audience participation. The regulars include people who have come to poetry late in life, perhaps for the first time, such as Steve Griffiths with his project *Late Love Poems,* as well as more seasoned writers like Gareth Owen who runs his own events, all glad of the chance to talk and think about poetry for a while. They include former documentary maker Marilyn Gaunt, who told me that when the last election did not go her preferred way, she wrote poems about it and posted them on trees and lampposts throughout the area. I just needed to do something, she said. Something in protest. Jean is also active in politics and we chatted on the street after she came back from a conference about poetry and climate change at the Free Word Centre in London. If they're asking the poets for help about climate change, she said darkly, we're all screwed.

---

[86] The Poetry Lounge, http://bit.ly/PoetryLudlow

Alongside these newer groups, older groups have been quietly meeting in Shropshire for a long time. The Salopian Poetry Society was formed in 1976, and involved making poetry pamphlets typed on a stencil, duplicated at the Dawley Information Centre and then stapled together on the chairwoman's kitchen table. These days they have 150 members and a 75-page magazine, as well as running an annual poetry competition. Another group, The Border Poets, have been going for about 20 years and meet 6-8 times a year, usually on a Sunday, for a day that apparently involves coffee and chat, poetry readings, a picnic and a visit to somewhere interesting for inspiration. The Arvon Foundation have a writing centre at The Hurst, playwright John Osborne's somewhat grim and imposing house in the Clun valley, drawing aspiring and established writers to their courses and newly refurbished stable block retreats. Their refurbishment has opened up the opportunity for the centre to feel part of the local community, with more gallery space and longer-term stays for writers meaning that there is a chance to engage with the locals rather than locking them away on course after course too intense for time to look beyond the walls of the house.

This is only a quick round-up, and I know I have missed people out, but what interests me is how a scene gets going in an area that seemingly doesn't have a lot going on on the surface. I moved to Ludlow after living in London for ten years, and at first glance you wonder how anything by way of culture can survive being so far away from anywhere else. It just didn't seem to me possible in such a remote area, without a critical mass of people or venues that seemed particularly driven or engaged. However, a few key personalities, all energised by their time and studies in bigger places – Birmingham, Keele, Manchester – in the right place at the right time all have enough impact between them to create a scene that lives and breathes and travels and writes. A lot of the groups overlap, with writers being part of several groups, and travelling the long distances needed to go to different events in different parts of the county for different occasions, but there is enough momentum to feel that, at the moment, Shropshire hills are once again filled with writers describing their contours and charms to audiences old and new. Perhaps one day the gift shops will catch up and replace the Housman quote with some new ideas.

14. MANIFESTO

Tony Walsh, Aka Longfella

'I don't know much about music; in my line of work you don't have to.'
– Elvis Presley

I've written poetry from the age of five, when my Nana, Queenie, would transcribe my earliest efforts into a treasured 1960s-styled notebook, using a red pen to write on its long, pink pages. It was at my Nan's also, aged 14 in 1979, listening in bed to John Peel's late night radio show on a tiny, tinny transistor radio, that I first heard 'Sonny's Lettah (Anti-Sus Poem)' by Jamaican dub poet Linton Kwesi Johnson. Packing a huge political, cultural and emotional punch, it hit me in the gut as hard as any piece of art has before or since. Together with the snap, crackle and be-bop-Beasley Street-cred of local hero, John Cooper Clarke, who knew that poetry could even do that? Could even be like that? Fucking wow!

As a music-mad kid, my first poets came disguised as lyricists: initially the likes of Paul Weller, Joe Strummer and Elvis Costello, but later along came Morrissey, Billy Bragg, Shane McGowan, Johnny Cash, Chuck D, Eric Bogle, Ewan MacColl, Mark E Smith, Bob Marley, Tracey Thorne, Terry Hall, Michael Franti, Christy Moore, Smokey Robinson, Gil Scott-Heron, Steve Earle, Patti Smith and a thousand other bedsit balladeers and manic street preachers. It took me a few years to work my way past the great punk myth that 1976 was a musical Year Zero, but I delved my way backwards: through Manchester's northern soul sounds into Motown, funk and blues; back through Two Tone and ska into dub and dancehall reggae; back from The Pogues into Irish and other folk musics; and back to the Hit Parades of the 50s, 60s and 70s, developing an appreciation of the (deceptively) simple, direct, affecting pop lyric. The early rappers – politicised and afro-centric, the terrace anthems of the Manchester scene, and the hands-in-the-air euphoria of the dance revolution all touched me deeply. The words and the music of the piece, working together to make you feel something. Folk music, all of it. Story telling. Connecting us. Mattering.

So when, in 2002/03, I wrote my first poems since my teens, now with a few of life's bruises, two small children and a terminally ill mother, this was my frame of reference. Not avant-garde or avant-meaning, avant-engagement, avant-got-a-clue-wot-you're-on-about-mate, stuff. But poetry that might hopefully get a hearing in the streets and pubs of my home town; poetry that would perhaps command the attention of music, comedy or theatre audiences; and poetry that could maybe, just maybe, change the mind of people expecting to be bored rigid. Often tightly rhymed and musically metred – we live our life to rhythms and patterns, we're hard-wired to receive them - but always trying to find a pulse or a heartbeat of some sort. Poems for the milkman to whistle; to make him laugh and cry when he caught the words.

So, when I first wandered nervously into Manchester to stutter my stuff in packed, tiny rooms above old-school boozers, I was thrilled to find that there were people who got my reference points, who shared my frustrations; and great local poets, rising out of the local open mic scene onto national and international stages, who would further inform and inspire my hopes of what poetry could be. Should be. What it once was and can be again.

Giving truth to the cliché, I'd found male and female, young and old, gay and straight, black and white, the skint and the solvent; poets of all shapes and surprises – sharing their stories, telling their truths and, mercifully, miraculously, minded to muse momentarily on me mumbling mine.

From under hoods and hijabs I heard them. From under fringes and 'fros, buzzcuts and bobs, from under green hair and grey, moptops and Mohawks, dreadlocks and… dreadful haircuts of all styles and none, I heard them. Shouting quietly, whispering loudly; killing me softly with - their poems. I'd found orators, creators and innovators whose dazzling diction and eclectic, electric rhetoric simply demanded my attention. A folk poetry, all of it. Story telling. Connecting us. Mattering.

Not here, the classical curricular canon of Shakespeare and Co. Not here, the freeform word-jazz of the pre-post-avant-neo-quasi-ExₚeЯi-

M3n☐aLi5t$. Not here even the so-called mainstream poetry which, sadly, is only mainstream if you mainly stream it from the private lakes and remote backwaters of our culture, causing barely a ripple outside of its own talent pool. Icy to those who might dare dip a toe. Not drowning, but not waving either.

No, not here. Here was… something else.

To my life-changing delight, I'd stumbled across a poetry as ancient as it is modern. A poetry that, whether knowingly or not, is rooted in the age-old traditions and folk memories that pre-date the written word. A vibrant, exciting poetry that borrows knowingly from hip-hop, reggae, punk and folk; that draws skilfully from theatre and stand-up comedy as well as from traditional poetic forms and techniques; that learns equally from the sacred and the profane, from the saucy postcard and the gospel hymn, from the fire and brimstone preacher, from pop culture and from the cultures of many lands. I'd found a poetry of patois, Punjabi and Polari; of jingles, jazz and jive; of minstrels, monologues and music halls. I'd found tub thumping, tongue twisting, truth telling troubadours; bombastic beat-boxing broadside balladeers; slam-tastic street corner soapbox slang slingers. I found an accessible, democratic People's Theatre, no less; unashamed to wear the masks of both comedy and tragedy, eschewing those of bafflement, boredom and blatantly bogus bourgeois belonging which are worn at all-too-many a poetry reading. Inclusive, not exclusive; fun, not funereal; sexy not sexless. Intelligent not unintelligible. But who knew that poetry could even do that? Could even be like that. Fucking wow!

So good luck, I say, to those who wish to continue wandering lonely as a cloud, my respect even. Just please don't presume to claim the whole art form as yours and yours alone. Other poetics are also available.

Here, sugaring 'the P word', re-branded as 'performance poetry', 'slam poetry', 'stand-up poetry', 'spoken word' and 'live literature', here were poetry events and poets, single poems even, that can take black consciousness, pink power, blue jokes and a green manifesto and wrap it all up in a red flag emblazoned with the golden words: *if we can't fucking dance it's not our revolution*! Marching fearlessly and unapologetically towards the true mainstream of our culture, ready to tattoo the hearts of anyone who will listen. 'Oi, Emperor! We can see your arse, mate!' We Have Come. To Spread. The Word!

Quiet girls turned Riot Grrrls. Bard to the bone. Poetry will never be 'the new rock and roll', they'll tell you, because it will always be the original rock and roll! 'Mad, bad and dangerous to know', they'll tell you. 'Peace and love'. 'Fight The Power'. Punk as fuck, even when disguised as librarians*.

(*Especially when disguised as librarians.)

Put simply, I'd found what I wanted to do with the rest of my life, what I have to do with the rest of my life. And, here I am, a few short years on from that first open mic night; I've given up a good day job, run away with the circus and I'm presenting many of my poems here on the page for the very first time.[87] If I'm honest, feeling more nervous and naked now than before any crowd, any classroom, any camera. I'm a 'performance poet', after all. 'It's the way I tell 'em', or so the dogma goes.

But I've been lucky enough to have been invited to poetry, literary and arts events of all kinds in recent years. I've witnessed many, and read too few, of the finest poets from the UK, North America and around the world. I've been privileged to study their forms and techniques, and observe their stage-craft and lack of it at close hand. But I still have so much to learn, there's nothing to be gained from ignorance or inverse snobbery. I take no misguided pride therefore in my own limited poetic apprenticeship; we should always remain as students. Indeed, along the way I've learned that many 'stage poets' could learn a lot in terms of craft and artistry from the best 'page poets' and vice versa in terms of connection and presentation, thereby making the whole art form stronger, growing the scene, widening and connecting the audiences.

But ultimately, I've learned that it's not about classical versus contemporary poetry, it's not about page versus stage, it's not about the raucous poetry slam versus the hushed reading, it's not about rhyme versus free verse, north versus south, or verses versus anything. Yes, there remain issues (count 'em!) around class, race, age, disability, gender and sexuality in the arts, as in so many walks of life. But, Jeez, I don't see anyone in our culture 'kicking against the pricks' harder or with more laser-guided, armour piercing wit and accuracy than our most socially engaged poets.

So, for me it's about communication – between poets, between poetries, with other artists and with new and strengthened audiences. It's about passion. It's about honesty. It's about the pursuit of truth and beauty. It's about poetry moving us to tears not boring us to tears. It's about entertainment value being admired not sneered at. It's about stopping

---

[87] This manifesto first appeared in my collection of poems *SEX & LOVE & ROCK&ROLL* (Burning Eye Books: Bristol, 2013)

attempts to reconcile the irreconcilable, stopping looking inwards, stopping the apologies for our art form and raising our game. It's about adopting the production values that modern audiences expect, reaching out to people young and old, and it's about 'most poetry ignoring most people' no longer. And it's about time.

So never mind the bollocks. Get on YouTube, get along to a local poetry night, and if there isn't one – or if you think that it's shit – then start your own. The internet means that it's never been easier to find great stuff, to connect with the people and scenes that interest you, to study your craft, study your craft, study your craft and to get your own stuff out there. You don't need anyone's permission. You don't need to find your path blocked by self-appointed and increasingly irrelevant gatekeepers – just go around them. You don't even need to know where you're heading, where this thing might take you, or what the so-called rules are.

You just need a pen, a page and a passion.

Go for it! Move mountains. Good luck!

ABOUT THE AUTHORS

MADIHA BATEINEH was previously a writer at the Office of Queen Rania in Jordan. She holds three Masters, including one in Creative Writing from Oxford University. An innovator, published writer, and creative leader, some of her work has been shortlisted and commended for Oxford's Martin Starkie Prize and the UK's National Poetry Competition. She has worked in various fields from journalism to government and is currently freelancing as she develops her own projects, which include a poetry collection entitled *The Lightworkers of Amman*. She loves ice cream (flavor depending on the season), illustrations and filling in her scrapbook, and listening to David Attenborough narrate the happenings of Planet Earth.

RACHEL BUCHANAN is a producer and arts manager based in Bristol. She is writing a book about her inventor stepfather and is training to be a Humanist Celebrant. Growing up in Shropshire is what first sent her travelling as far as she could, although now she knows there are few more beautiful places in the world. @rachelonthehill

EMMA LEE's most recent collection is *Ghosts in the Desert* (IDP, 2015) and she was co-editor for *Over Land, Over Sea: poems for those seeking refuge* (Five Leaves, 2015). She reviews for poetry journals and blogs at http://emmalee1.wordpress.com.

MAAKOMELE R. MANAKA is a Soweto born poet with a strong artistic heritage. Mak, as he is widely known, has published three collections of poetry: *If Only, In Time* and *Flowers of a Broken Smile*, many of Manaka's poems have been translated into Italian and German. His writings have appeared in literary journals and newspapers around the country, *Mail & Guardian, Aerodrome, New Coin, Botsotso, Kotaz, The Chronic* and *Poetry Potion*. He also recorded a dub-poetry album titled, *Word Sound Power*. Manaka has been invited to perform his poetry at various literary festivals locally and abroad, from Soweto to Spain, Cuba, Jamaica, Lesotho, Botswana, Germany, Holland, Italy, Switzerland, and at the inauguration of former president Thabo Mbeki. He also performed for the late Nelson Mandela. He has been nominated for The Daimler Chrysler Poet of The Year 2005 Award, and has represented South Africa at the closing ceremony of the 2006 FIFA World Cup in Germany. Manaka runs creative writing classes in and around South Africa, and he holds a Masters Degree in Creative Writing from Rhodes University.

RACHEL MCCRUM worked as a poet, performer and promoter in Edinburgh from 2012 until 2017, arriving via Manchester, Belfast, New Zealand, Oxford and a small seaside town in Northern Ireland. She was Broad of Rally & Broad, organisers of a popular Edinburgh-based 'poetry cabaret'. She has performed and taught workshops in poetry and performance in Greece, South Africa, Haiti and around the UK. In August 2015 she wrote and performed her first solo show at the Edinburgh Fringe, as part of new spoken word collective SHIFT/. Also in 2015 she was Writer in Residence for CoastWord, Dunbar, and the inaugural BBC Scotland Poet in Residence. McCrum's first pamphlet, *The Glassblower Dances*, published by Stewed Rhubarb Press, was the winner of the 2012 Callum Macdonald Memorial Award. In 2017, Freight published her first full-length collection *The First Blast to Awaken Degenerate Women*.

SHARON MOREHAM is an alumni of the International School of Storytelling (UK) and co-founder of *The Story Collective*, a community group exploring the use of oral storytelling to develop human potential and wellbeing in Ōtautahi Christchurch, Aotearoa New Zealand, where she currently lives. Sharon has worked in various fields including health, government and community sectors but is now turning her hand to freelancing, following her own creative projects, and somehow squeezing in further study. She is currently undertaking a Masters of Indigenous Studies at the University of Otago, exploring the meaning of belonging in a bi-cultural Māori-Pākeha family and society, and oral traditions and historical narratives of the Pacific.

MARTÍN RANGEL is a Mexican writer, poet, wordsmith, translator, and internet-artist. He is the author of several books, including *Rojo* (2013), *El rugido leve: las canciones de Ryan Karazija* (2015), *emoji de algo muerto* (2015). *delirioamateur* (2016) and *Al margen del mundo* (2017). He raps, speaks, performs and publishes net-collages and glitch art as "R V N G E L" and produces experimental electronic music and "sound art" as "MALVIAJE". https://martinrangel.tumblr.com/ https://martinrangel.bandcamp.com/

LAWRENCE SCHIMEL is a bilingual author & translator based in Madrid, Spain. His most book is a collection of 100 erotic microfiction in Spanish, *Una barba para dos* (Dos Bigotes), and his recent translations include *Nothing is Lost: Selected Poems* by Jordi Doce (Shearsman) and the novel *The Wild Book* by Juan Villoro (Restless Books).

NG YI-SHENG is a Singaporean writer and LGBT activist. His books include his debut poetry collection *last boy*, which won the Singapore Literature Prize, the best-selling *SQ21*, the movie novelisation *Eating Air* and the spoken word collection *Loud Poems for a Very Obliging Audience*. He tweets and Instagrams at @yishkabob.

SCHEREZADE SIOBHAN is an award-winning Indo-Rroma Jungian scarab turned psychologist, mental health advocate, community catalyst, and a writer. Her work has appeared in international journals, anthologies, art exhibits, theater performances and bios of OkCupid users. She is the author of a chapbook, *Bone Tongue* (Thought Catalog Books, 2015), a full-length poetry collection, *Father, Husband,* (Salopress UK), poetry pamphlet, *to dhikr, i* (Pyramid Editions, forthcoming) & her next second full length collection *The Bluest Kaliis* scheduled for release in 2018 (Lithic Press, USA). She is the creator and curator of *The Mira Project*, a global dialogue on women's mental health, gendered violence, and street harassment and also runs *Bruja Roja* - a literary space dedicated to publishing arrangements of language, art and journalism by women, non-binary, trans, queer & neurodiverse people. She can be found squeeing about militant bunnies at @zaharaesque on twitter/fb/IG.

CLAIRE TRÉVIEN is the author of *The Shipwrecked House* (Penned in the Margins, 2013), which was the reader's choice in the Guardian's First Book Awards. It was subsequently turned into a one-woman multimodal show and toured the UK. Her other books include *Astéronymes* (Penned in the Margins, 2016) and *Satire, Prints and Theatricality in the French Revolution* (Oxford University Studies in the Enlightenment, 2016). She founded Sabotage Reviews and runs its annual Saboteur Awards. More blah can be found at clairetrevien.co.uk or you can tell her to stop complaining about train delays at @CTrevien

BBC Slam Champion SOPHIA WALKER is an internationally renowned poet and teaching artist. Her spoken word shows have toured through theatres in the UK and internationally to critical acclaim, winning Best UK Spoken Word Show 2014 at the Saboteur Awards, and the awards for Best Spoken Word Show on the Edinburgh Free Fringe in 2013 and 2014. Her debut collection *Opposite the Tourbus* was published by Burning Eye Press in 2014. Most recently, she co-founded The Spoken Word Theatre Foundation.

TONY WALSH, also known as Longfella, is the author of *Sex & Love & Rock&Roll* (Burning Eye Books, 2015). In May 2017, he went viral after delivering his poem "This Is the Place" to the crowds gathered in Albert Square in central Manchester for the public vigil following the bomb attack at the Manchester Arena. www.longfella.co.uk @LongfellaPoet

CATHERINE WILSON is a spoken word poet from Edinburgh. She is one of the organisers of *Loud Poets*: a collective of artists, writers and musicians committed to making poetry interesting to everyone. Whilst at the University of Edinburgh she ran both the open mic *Soapbox*, and Scotland's largest free slam. She was an organiser and member of the University of Edinburgh's winning poetry team at *UniSlam* and the *Hammer and Tongue Team Slam*, who were also the first non-American team to compete at C.U.P.S.I. in Austin, 2016. She has performed internationally and across the U.K., and written with organisations including *The National Gallery, The National Museum*, the *BBC, StAnza Poetry Festival* and *TEDx*.

ALICE S. YOUSEF is a Palestinian translator, blogger, and emerging poet, who has published short stories and translations. Her work can be found on web-magazines including *Twopoetswrite* and *VisualVerse*. She holds a Masters in Writing from Warwick University and is a fellow of the University of Iowa's International Writing Program. She tweets @Aliceyousef. http://bloomsnindigo.blogspot.com/

27620418R10070

Printed in Great Britain
by Amazon

Use this space for your words....

Printed in Great Britain
by Amazon